P9-CDW-805

A Time to Every Purpose

A Time to Every Purpose

letters to a young jew

JONATHAN D. SARNA

BASIC
BOOKS

A Member of the Perseus Books Group
New York

Copyright © 2008 by Jonathan D. Sarna
Published by Basic Books, A Member of the Perseus Books Group

Books published by Basic Books are available at special discounts for bulk purchases in the United States by corporations, institutions, and other organizations. For more information, please contact the Special Markets Department at the Perseus Books Group, 2300 Chestnut Street, Suite 200, Philadelphia, PA 19103, or call (800) 810-4145, ext. 5000, or e-mail special.markets@perseusbooks.com.

Library of Congress Cataloging-in-Publication Data
Sarna, Jonathan D.
    A time to every purpose : letters to a young Jew / Jonathan D. Sarna.
      p. cm.
    Includes bibliographical references and index.
    ISBN 978-0-465-00246-7 (alk. paper)
    1. Fasts and feasts—Judaism. 2. Philosophy, Jewish. 3. Judaism. I. Title.

BM690.S3144 2008
296.7—dc22

                                                            2008015413

10 9 8 7 6 5 4 3 2 1

To the memory of my Sarna and Horowitz ancestors.

"Fortunate is the person whose ancestors
have accrued for him merit."

—Jerusalem Talmud,
Berachot 4:1, 7d (47b)

CONTENTS

A NOTE ON TRANSLITERATION
FROM HEBREW

This book transliterates Hebrew words according to the rules laid down in the *Encyclopaedia Judaica*. Those interested in learning more about a particular subject can usually find an entry in the encyclopedia under the same spelling. The only tricky feature of the transliteration system is the unfamiliar letter ḥ. This represents the Hebrew letter *ḥet*, the eighth letter of the Hebrew alphabet. It stands at the head of such words as Ḥanukkah and is pronounced gutturally like the final letter in the German name *Bach*.

A NOTE ON
THE JEWISH CALENDAR

The Jewish calendar, unlike its more familiar counterpart, the Gregorian calendar, harmonizes the monthly waxing and waning of the moon with the annual revolution of the earth around the sun. Each month in the Jewish calendar begins with the appearance of the new moon and lasts for a full lunar cycle (29–30 days). Since twelve lunar months amount to only 354 days, whereas a solar year is 365 days, the Jewish calendar adds a "leap month" just prior to spring, seven times in nineteen years, so as to reconcile the lunar and the solar cycles. In leap years there are two months named Adar, known, rather unimaginatively, as Adar I and Adar II. The leap month ensures that the holiday of Passover, the festival of spring, remains fixed in its proper season, always falling between late March and late April.

The names of the months in the Jewish calendar are as follows:

NAME OF MONTH	LENGTH	GREGORIAN EQUIVALENT
1 Nisan	30 days	March–April
2 Iyar	29 days	April–May
3 Sivan	30 days	May–June
4 Tammuz	29 days	June–July
5 Av	30 days	July–August
6 Elul	29 days	August–September
7 Tishri	30 days	September–October
8 Ḥeshvan	29 or 30 days	October–November
9 Kislev	30 or 29 days	November–December
10 Tevet	29 days	December–January
11 Shevat	30 days	January–February
12[a] Adar I	30 days	February–March
12[b] Adar	29 days	February–March

a. Leap years only.
b. In leap years, this is month 13 and called Adar II.

New Jewish calendars are usually published in the fall to coincide with Rosh Hashanah, the Jewish new year. Nevertheless, the first month in the Jewish year, according to the Book of Exodus, is Nisan, because that is when the Exodus from Egypt took place. A helpful website where one can explore 9,999 years of the Jewish calendar, translate dates back and forth between Jewish and Gregorian years, and see when Jewish holidays fall in any year may be found at http://www.hebcal.com.

PREFACE

The great folksinger Pete Seeger was thumbing through his Bible one day, and the words of Ecclesiastes jumped out at him: "To every thing there is a season and a time to every purpose under heaven." Seeger turned those words into a famous folksong (*Turn, Turn, Turn*) that became an anthem of the 1960s and a recurrent hit ever since.

Long before then, however, the Jewish calendar promoted the very same idea: a time to every purpose. To understand what Judaism is, one must experience the laughter and the tears, the teachings and the memories, the hopes and the fears that characterize the Jewish holiday cycle. The Jewish holidays, from Passover to Purim, illustrate the central themes of Jewish life. To each there is a season.

The thirteen letters to my daughter that form the heart of this book examine these central themes through the prism of the Jewish holiday cycle. Each letter begins with a particular holiday and takes the reader on a journey from the origins of that holiday to the great issues that it illuminates. Some letters consider new observances like

Holocaust Remembrance Day and Israel Independence Day. Others recall little-known days, like Tu be-Av, a holiday celebrating love and marriage. Together, they address major topics of concern to young Jews today, including intermarriage, identity, assimilation, antisemitism, freedom, Torah, Israel, social justice, the Holocaust, the environment, continuity, and happiness.

This book assumes that the more one *experiences* Judaism, the more one appreciates what Judaism is. No letter addresses the question, so popular in Jewish circles today, "*Why* be Jewish?" As I see it, Judaism is not so much a "why" as a way: a way of life; a way of marking time and sanctifying space; a way of relating to family, to history, and to the environment; a way of thinking about God, Torah, and Israel.

The goal of this volume is to introduce "young" Jews (as far as I can tell, Jews are eternally "young" until that stupefying moment when, without warning, they declare themselves "old"), as well as non-Jews who may be interested in Judaism, to the major holidays of the Jewish calendar and the major themes of contemporary Jewish life. As an academic, I am beholden to no particular movement in Jewish life, and this book therefore offers no brief for any particular movement, save for Judaism itself. It represents my own views on various contested issues, along with other points of view. *Maḥloket*—disputation— is to my mind central to the Jewish tradition. My aim here is not to make decisions for readers, but rather to help them make wise and well-informed decisions for themselves.

THIS BOOK MARKS a onetime departure from the usual works of American Jewish history that I produce. Lara Heimert, who had been my editor at Yale University Press and has now moved up to Basic Books, persuaded me to undertake this task. George Weigel's lyrical *Letters to a Young Catholic* provided the inspiration for this book and the sense that undertaking it would be worthwhile.

I am grateful to friends and relatives from across the spectrum of Jewish life who read and commented on this volume, improving it in innumerable ways. Rachel Frankel, Rabbi William Hamilton, Rabbi Zachary Heller, Scott-Martin Kosofsky, Ellen Smith, and Rabbi Martin Weiner all took time out from their busy schedules to read this book in draft. So did my wife, Professor Ruth Langer, my brother, David E. Y. Sarna, and my daughter, Leah Livia Sarna.

I addressed the letters in this book to Leah with her permission, and her comments and criticisms proved invaluable to me. Watching her and her older brother, Aaron, prepare to leave home and make their own way in the Jewish community inspired me to write *A Time to Every Purpose*. May it help my children, and all my readers, to appreciate the Jewish calendar, understand and confront the myriad challenges facing contemporary Jews, and lead more purpose-driven lives.

A Time to Every Purpose

FREEDOM

Passover

Dear Leah,

The "Today in History" column in this morning's *Boston Globe* reminds me that in "1783, on this date [April 11], Congress proclaimed the cessation of hostilities with Great Britain." That day, perhaps more even than July Fourth, secured our nation's freedom. How fitting that the anniversary of the Revolutionary War's conclusion falls this year on the eve of Passover! A pity that this does not happen every year.

We have been consumed with Passover preparations over these past weeks. Every year, it seems, we relive at this time our people's epic journey from slavery to freedom as recounted in the Bible. Ima insists that every room in the house, even those that we hardly use, be thoroughly cleaned for Passover, so we have been scrubbing every night. As for my study, I have been chained here for two full days putting my books and papers in order and cleaning up all of the stray raisins and M&Ms

that found their way into cracks and crevices. "Remove leaven from your houses," the Bible proclaims, and as a faithful servant I dutifully comply. Cleaning the house from top to bottom, changing over all the dishes, and filling the cupboards with "kosher for Passover" foods free from all leavening agents is physically exhausting. So are the preparations for tonight's big seder, where we shall be fifteen around the table. But once Ima lights the candles ushering in the holiday, I shall finally be a free man. The weeks of self-styled "enslavement" render the experience of freedom all the more sweet.

"Slaves were we to Pharoah in Egypt and God brought us out from there"—so the traditional seder liturgy known as the haggadah teaches. The haggadah forges a link between past and present. The goal is to re-live history, to re-experience the movement from slavery to freedom, to *personally* undergo the Exodus from Egypt.

That explains the special foods that we eat at the Passover seder. Matzah, made only from flour and water in a process that must hastily be completed within eighteen minutes, reminds us that there was no time to bake bread upon leaving Egypt. Bitter herbs, usually sharp horseradish or tart lettuce, recall the bitterness of slave life. Ḥaroset, a mixture of nuts, wine, spices, and fruit, symbolizes the mortar that the Israelites produced during their enslavement, when they were forced to make bricks.

Some Jews recline on pillows during the seder as if to vaunt their liberation, their pride in being free men and women. Others physically reenact the Exodus, miming both the suffering of the slave and the joys of emancipation. Perhaps only those who have experienced slavery themselves can truly appreciate the meaning of freedom, but each of us must try.

You ASKED ME, a few weeks ago, whether the Exodus actually happened. Can the biblical story—the enslavement of the Israelites, Moses challenging Pharoah, the ten plagues, the crossing of the Red Sea, the forty years in the wilderness, the giving of the Torah, and the triumphant entry into the land of Israel—be conclusively verified? Opinions are mixed. (Why aren't you surprised?) The absence of any archaeological evidence of a large migration through the desert, and the fact that extensive research at major cities like Jericho shows no evidence of the kind of destruction the Bible describes, suggest to some scholars that the whole story is a myth. Other scholars, however, point to the large number of details in the Bible that can be verified historically. They insist that there is abundant archaeological evidence showing that newcomers did arrive in the land of Israel just when the Bible says they did. Besides, they ask, why would anyone have invented a tradition that their ancestors were "interlopers with a humiliating background as slaves"?

Not being a biblical scholar myself, I have always found questions like this perplexing. First of all, the Bible as I read it never claims to be a history book; it teaches above all moral and religious lessons. Second, how could one possibly hope to prove or disprove most of the events that the Bible recounts, especially since it sometimes tells the same story several different ways?

Since we can never know exactly what happened 3,300 years ago, I think it is more important to affirm that the Exodus plays an absolutely critical role in Jewish memory. The story lives within us. Not only is it referenced over and over in the Bible and in Jewish prayers, but even major holidays and the Sabbath are explained as being "in remembrance of the departure from Egypt." Ethical lessons too derive from the Exodus. "You shall not wrong a stranger or oppress him," the Bible teaches, "for you were strangers in the land of Egypt." When you harvest, it continues, leave behind gleanings for widows, orphans, and strangers to gather up, for "always remember that you were a slave in the land of Egypt." Down to our very day, the Exodus story continues to inspire movements of social justice around the world. The oppressed recall and echo Moses' simple, passionate plea: "Let my people go."

Regardless of whether the story happened precisely as the Bible recounts, the consequences of the Exodus have been incalculable. Reading the story anew each year in the Passover haggadah inevitably calls to mind the whole sweep of Jewish history, along with many comparable liberation movements, including the American Revolution. Anyone who has ever moved from being unfree to being free can understand what Passover means. Benjamin Franklin even sought to depict the liberation from Egypt on the seal of the United States, along with the motto "Rebellion to Tyrants Is Obedience to God."

Back when Ima was a girl, she used a haggadah produced by her grandfather's rabbi, Dr. J. Leonard Levy of Pittsburgh, that made that link between Jewish freedom and American freedom explicit. Levy's was a nontraditional haggadah that called for the placement of an American flag on the seder table and included the following memorable dialogue as part of its ritual:

CHILD: *Where do we find civil, political, and religious liberty united today?*

READER: *Here in America. The fathers of this country fought against oppression that here all men should be free and equal before the law; free to worship God as their conscience dictated. To us the United States of America stands as the foremost among nations, granting the greatest liberty to all who dwell here. Therefore we grace our table with the National flag. . . .*

The Pilgrim Fathers landed here inspired by Israel's wandering to go out even to the wilderness and worship God. The immortal Declaration of Independence is the Great Charter announced before Pharaoh by Moses. The Abolitionists are the product of the Bible, and the love of civil liberty that moved [William Ellery] Channing and [Theodore] Parker, [John Greenleaf] Whittier and [William] Lloyd Garrison was nourished by it. The Old Testament first taught men that Government must be a government by law equally applicable to all, and this is the controlling idea of Mosaic and American legislation. The Fourth of July is the American Passover. Thanksgiving is the American Feast of Tabernacles.

It is therefore quite in keeping with the service this evening to pledge our country. In raising this third glass of wine to our lips, let us pray that God will ever protect our land, that here liberty may forever dwell, that peace may abide within her borders and prosperity within her homes.

Levy died at fifty-one in the great flu pandemic, just weeks after Passover in 1917. But the valiant effort to connect the holiday of freedom to the land of freedom by no means ended with him. To this day, many Jews in the United States conclude the Passover seder with the singing of the hymn, *America*.

Haggadahs here in America and everywhere nowadays come in all shapes and sizes. There are thousands upon thousands of different editions, the oldest dating back to the tenth century. To turn the pages of these well-used books is to reflect upon the Jewish people's rich diversity, the wide range of communities that Jews have inhabited. There are handwritten haggadahs and printed haggadahs, Hebrew haggadahs and translated haggadahs, haggadahs that preserve the traditional text and haggadahs that modify the traditional text, haggadahs with multiple commentaries and no illustrations, and haggadahs with multiple illustrations and no commentaries. Perhaps the best known haggadah of all is the simple Maxwell House haggadah, produced by the famous coffeemaker since 1934. Some fifty million copies of that edition have reputedly been distributed.

There is, then, an haggadah for every Jew: unorthodox and orthodox, conservative and radical, religious and secular, even one for strict vegetarians. All of them tell essentially the same Passover story, but they do so in different ways, at different lengths, in different languages, and with somewhat different contemporary messages. Everyone can select the haggadah that they find most meaningful. Considering that Passover is the holiday of freedom, what could be more appropriate?

FREEDOM, OF COURSE, means different things to different people. To us, freedom means personal liberty, the freedom to choose. The more choices, the better. That's why America boasts a wide variety of Jews, almost as many varieties as there are of haggadahs! There are Orthodox, Conservative, Reform, and Reconstructionist Jews; trans-denominational and postdenominational Jews; Hasidic, Havurah, and humanistic Jews; Polydox Jews; Renewal Jews; secular Jews; and plenty of Jews who define themselves as "just Jewish" or "other." Within these movements, there are also endless choices: lots of ways of being Conservative or Reform, lots of different Hasidic sects, lots of . . . well, you get the idea.

Freedom, many Americans believe, means picking and choosing one's way through Judaism, selecting cafeteria-style from its bountiful offerings, creating one's own way of being Jewish, a Judaism that is personally meaningful. The result? There are almost as many Judaisms as there are Jews. Not everybody likes that, but it is the price we pay for religious freedom.

Given the reality of choice, how should *you* decide what kind of Jew to become?

Sorry, but you will have to figure that out for yourself. I would not even try to make the decision for you. You would be sorely disappointed, though, if I did not offer at least a few suggestions, so here goes:

You might decide based on your religious priorities.

Different people have different priorities when it comes to faith. Some consider it most important to uphold and maintain Judaism's sacred religious traditions. Others seek to adapt Judaism to new conditions of life in the communities where they live. Still others desire, above all, to preserve a strong sense of Jewish peoplehood and communal unity. Most Jewish movements actually cherish all three of these essential values, but they each have different priorities and emphases. What are yours?

You might decide based on family traditions.

Think about how you have seen Judaism practiced in our home, among our relatives on both sides, and in the various synagogues we have joined. What seems most familiar and comfortable to you? What gives you the satisfying sense that you are following in the traditions of our ancestors?

You might decide based on what moves you spiritually.

Are you particularly stirred by a certain kind of prayer experience? A particular kind of music? Clapping and dancing? Hand-holding and hugging? Don't be afraid to listen to your heart and your soul.

You might decide based on your beliefs and passions.

What particularly excites you about Judaism: Adherence to Jewish law (*halacha*)? Love of Torah and learning? A commitment to Israel and to the Jewish people? Making the world a better place for everyone? How about pursuing all of these goals at once? Let your beliefs guide you.

You might decide based on the kind of community that you want for yourself and your family.

Are you looking to join a community that shares similar commitments and orientations? A caring community where people support one another? A community where everyone lives within close proximity? A warm, homogeneous community? An amazingly diverse community? If, after diligently searching, you cannot find a community that shares the Judaism of your dreams, remember that there is always another option. You could gather together a few of your friends and create a community of your own.

WHATEVER YOU DECIDE, I hope that you will learn as much as you can about Judaism's teachings and practices. Consider your heritage a precious resource and explore its multiple dimensions. Let our rich and beautiful traditions inform your life choices, guiding you in all that you do as you shape your own life and strive to improve the lives of those around you.

Learning Hebrew is valuable here, because so many of Judaism's primary sources were originally written in Hebrew. Hebrew is the language that has bound Jews together historically and that is spoken in the contemporary state of Israel. Diaspora Jewish languages like Aramaic, the language of most Jews in the early centuries of the Common Era; Yiddish, the Germanic language once spoken by most Central and Eastern European Jews; and Ladino, the Spanish counterpart to Yiddish used by many Jews with roots in the Iberian peninsula, were likewise suffused with Hebrew and usually written in Hebrew letters. A knowledgeable Jew, therefore, needs to know Hebrew.

But even without knowing a word of Hebrew, you can still study most of the primary texts and sources of Judaism in translation. The Bible, the Talmud, the writings of Moses Maimonides, the mystical Zohar, the standard prayer book, the haggadah, and many other Jewish classics have been published in English and a range of other languages. The library of Jewish books is immense, filled with volumes of law and lore; history, biography, philosophy, theology, and mysticism; contemporary Jewish life; and fiction and poetry and fantasy. The more you learn, the more you will want to learn, and the more you'll appreciate Judaism's diversity and richness. Being better informed will also help you to decide what kind of Jew to become.

Being a knowledgeable Jew, though, is not enough. I hope that you will also think about becoming a practicing Jew. Judaism, at its core, is a religion of actions and deeds. Helping the needy, visiting the sick, comforting the bereaved, lighting Sabbath candles, keeping kosher, making a Passover seder—these are among the practices (observant Jews would say "commandments" or *mitsvot)* that give substance to Jewish life. There are myriad ways of practicing Judaism: 613 traditional commandments and thousands upon thousands of customs. Try a few. I have always found that "doing Jewish" actively is infinitely more satisfying than "being Jewish" passively.

Speaking of "doing Jewish," I have to get back to preparing for tonight's seder. Our guests come from different places, and they have different traditions that I want to respect. The vegetables that we dip? You remember that our family uses parsley for the ritual, but one of our guests prefers celery, and another says that his family has *always* used potatoes—and they claim to be descended from King David! I won't tell him this, but actually Spanish explorers brought the potato from Peru to Europe in the sixteenth century; King David never ate a potato in his life! The potato custom actually developed when Jews lived in cold climates where green vegetables were not to be found at Passover time. Still, family customs are not to be trifled with. A potato he shall have.

There are other traditions that guests are bringing with them. One discovered a custom, dating back to the early Middle Ages, of adding fish to the seder table in commemoration of Miriam, the sister of Moses. According to the interpretation she showed me, the meat on the seder plate recalls Moses, the egg recalls Aaron, and the fish recalls Miriam—together they led Israel out of bondage. Another guest, meanwhile, wants to include "Miriam's cup" alongside the traditional Elijah's cup. Miriam's cup is filled with pure water—a reminder of the rabbinic legend concerning "Miriam's well," a wondrous rock that, according to one tradition, miraculously dispensed water on demand during the Israelites' forty years in the desert. Although neither of these customs was known to my father, Sabba, whose traditions I have generally followed, I want our guests to feel welcomed and comfortable tonight. Besides, new customs will presumably generate new questions—and that, in a sense, is what the seder is all about.

SABBA HIMSELF introduced a new custom into the seder. Amazing that you still remember this—what an impression it must have made upon you as a young child! He always recited a solemn prayer in the middle of the seder, right before we open the door to welcome in the prophet Elijah. He insisted that we all stand for its recitation.

Composed in the 1950s, the prayer commemorates the 1943 Warsaw Ghetto uprising, which began on Passover eve. Sabba knew survivors of that uprising. Warsaw once had the largest Jewish community in Europe: some 375,000 Jews lived there on the eve of World War II. The Nazis, when they captured Poland, confined those Jews to a tiny ghetto surrounded by a high wall. People lived six or seven to a room. By the time of the uprising, most Jews had already died of starvation and disease or been transported to death camps. But the more than 50,000 who remained courageously battled the Nazis when they came to liquidate the ghetto. Using primitive weapons and fighting from underground bunkers, they held off the Nazis for weeks. Most eventually perished, but the courage that they displayed inspires us still. My eyes moisten now when I think of the last words of the prayer that Sabba always recited:

And from the depths of their affliction, the martyrs lifted their voices in a song of faith in the coming of the Messiah, when justice and brotherhood will reign . . .

And then we all joined together in singing the plaintive song that those martyrs sang:

I believe with perfect faith in the coming of the
> *Messiah:*
And though he tarry, none the less do I believe!

This theme—messianic redemption (understood by different Jews in different ways), the coming of God's kingdom, the anticipation of a better future—fits perfectly with the message of Passover. "In every generation," the haggadah declares, "people rise against us to destroy us, but the Holy One saves us from their hand." The closing hymn at the end of many contemporary haggadahs—the Aramaic song *Ḥad Gadya*—concludes with God slaying the angel of death. The end of the classical haggadah, before the later songs were added, closes on a similar note (forgive the bad poetry of the English translation; the original Hebrew is better):

We've made another Seder just as we were told.
We followed all the rules laid down in days of old.
As we were worthy to order it here,
So may we do it again next year!
Pure One who dwells in the heavens above,
Restore your countless people, bring them home with
> *love;*

Take quickly Your vine shoots and replant them
    strong
Back in Zion's vineyard, where they will sing your
    song.
Next year in Jerusalem!

Perhaps, in the end, this message is the link between the Exodus from Egypt, the end of the American Revolution, and the Warsaw Ghetto uprising, all of which we recall tonight at the seder. It is not just that all three reflect the quest for freedom, however differently defined, but that all exemplify the quest for a better life, a better world, and a better tomorrow. The uplifting message of Passover, one that has sustained Jews through the centuries and will, I trust, sustain you too, comes down finally to hope.

Happy Passover!

Love,
Abba

FOOD, FAMILY, AND JEWISH DISTINCTIVENESS

Maimuna

Dear Leah,

Hope that you had a lovely seder. You sure were missed here!

Last night, Passover ended. All the special Passover dishes are now back in storage, and the house has returned more or less to its normal state. But whereas most years, I rush off to the supermarket right after Passover to buy bread, this year I did something altogether different. A Moroccan acquaintance invited me to join him at his house for what he called "Maimuna," and I took him up on the offer.

Growing up, I did not know any Moroccan Jews and was only dimly aware that there was a Jewish community in Morocco at all. I certainly did not know that it once numbered two hundred and fifty thousand and traced its roots back to the time of the Israelite kings, long before the rise of Christianity and Islam. Sadly, the Moroccan

Jewish community, like all of its counterparts in Arab lands, experienced growing persecution after the establishment of the State of Israel. As a result, the community dispersed, with most Jews fleeing to Israel, France, or North America. Fewer than three thousand Jews remain in Morocco today. Wherever they live, Moroccan Jews fondly recall the world they left behind—especially on Maimuna.

Maimuna is a rollicking springtime festival that begins for Moroccan Jews as soon as Passover concludes. My host tells me that it is named for Maimon, the father of the great Jewish scholar Moses Maimonides, who for a time lived in the Moroccan city of Fez. An article I read disagrees, claiming that it is actually named for a mythical demon named Maimun, whom the festival seeks to appease. A friend who knows Arabic snorted at both explanations. Maimuna, she says, comes from the Arabic word meaning wealth, plenty, and good fortune.

Whatever the case, Maimuna today focuses on eating and socializing. At David's house, trays of freshly baked pita bread flew out of the oven—a particularly delicious way of satiating my post-Passover cravings. Relatives dipped the flat bread in honey and butter as a sign of family togetherness. The bread was followed by a banquet of fish and dairy delicacies—no meat is allowed. The specialty of the house is *muflita*, a sweet crepe-like pancake made of fried dough. There was also a popular pudding called *zabane* that tastes a bit like caramel. Late into the night, friends and relatives dropped by the house to eat, drink, gossip, and sing.

In Israel, the household celebration at night is followed by a day of picnics and beach parties with lots of singing and dancing, along with courting and matchmaking. Back in Morocco, I am told, houses were decorated with greenery as a sign of spring, and young people dressed up in Arab garb and toured the streets with mandolins, exchanging blessings. The festival, back then, engaged Jews with the Muslim majority among whom they lived, even as it expressed Jews' fervent hope for redemption from exile.

What struck me, seeing Maimuna for the first time, was how closely interwoven the festival is to three central aspects of Jewish life that extend far beyond Morocco. These three themes—food, family, and Jewish distinctiveness—seem to me to underlie much of Jewish life as we know it.

Like most groups, we Jews have historically defined ourselves by our food selections. We are what we eat, and not just at Maimuna. There are special foods, like matzah, that we eat on Passover. There are other foods, like the braided bread known as hallah, that we eat on the Sabbath. Then there are foods, like chicken soup (also known as Jewish penicillin), that our sages considered good for our health and that passed into our regular diet.

Many of the foods that you grew up thinking were "Jewish foods," like bagels and lox, blintzes, knishes, and

kugel, actually are characteristic only of particular re-
gions where Jews lived; they are as strange to my Moroccan Jewish friends as their foods are to me. But other
foods, like the slow-cooking stew that Eastern European
Jews call *cholent* and Sephardic Jews call *hamin,* turn up in
different varieties around the Jewish world. Since cook-
ing on the Sabbath is prohibited, foods that can be prepared in advance and kept hot have served an essential
ritual purpose.

Jewish law sets forth an entire series of other regulations and taboos that have shaped Jewish food and distin-
guished Jews from their neighbors. These, as you know,
are the laws that define whether food is kosher. Years ago,
when I was in the hospital, one of the nurses brought me
a bowl of soup and assured me that she had removed all
the pork so "it was safe for me to eat." She thought that
keeping kosher meant no more than abstaining from
pork and bacon! Of course, the rules are much more
complicated than that.

For one thing, keeping kosher means separating milk
from meat, a requirement that the rabbis deduced from
the Bible. Traditional Jews have two completely different
sets of dishes and cutlery (and some have two different
dishwashers as well) to ensure that nothing associated
with meat touches anything associated with dairy. No
washing down hot dogs with a glass of milk!

In addition, keeping kosher means eating only foods
certified as being kosher, such as meat from approved

animals and birds that have been specially slaughtered and salted, fish with fins and scales (no oysters, no lobsters), and processed foods free of all non-kosher ingredients. Most people who keep kosher do not study the vast array of biblically derived rules and regulations for themselves. Instead, they look for symbols like O-U or O-K on their food packages, which indicate that the food is under rabbinic supervision and is therefore *really* safe for them to eat.

I know folks who think that kosher food is so pure and holy that it will actually keep you healthy. The Food and Drug Administration, however, is unlikely to agree. In fact, not even the Bible makes any such claim! Instead, the point of kosher food, even in ancient times, was to make Jews feel distinctive and special. Lots of world religions, including Islam, Hinduism, and Mormonism, set their members apart through conspicuous food practices. Inevitably, such rules separate insiders from outsiders, those who are faithful from those who are not. Had it not been for their distinctive food rules, a small minority group like the Jews would probably long ago have assimilated out of existence.

Keeping kosher is a big decision. It changes the way you eat and limits what you eat (no bacon or cheeseburgers, ever!). It can be especially challenging away from home, where kosher restaurants are scarce. Just as one of your friend's diets defines her as a vegan, keeping kosher defines you as a Jew. It establishes a relationship between you, your family, and the traditions of the Jewish people.

SPEAKING OF FAMILY, what impressed me at the Maimuna celebration was the centrality of family ties, another critical factor in Jewish survival. Most of the folks I met were related to one another, and they interacted much the way we do at big family gatherings. Some came dressed to the nines; others were clearly quite poor; a number departed as soon as they could; and one or two played an obviously central role: they exchanged passionate greetings with everybody! All alike acknowledged commitment to family as a sacred obligation.

So it is, I think, among the Jewish people as a whole. The idea that all Jews are related to one another—that we are one big family—is one of the most audacious ideas in Jewish life. Imagine, millions of relatives: rich, poor, learned, ignorant, happy, sad, religious, irreligious, likable, dislikable—and all of them family. Instead of the nuclear family that we so narrowly focus upon, Jewish peoplehood celebrates an extended Jewish family. It relates us back in time to every Jew who has ever lived since Abraham and Sarah in the Bible, and it relates us across space to every Jew alive today.

Does this mean that we are the chosen people? The Bible boldly states that we are. The idea that Jews are a distinct and chosen people is emphatically stated:

You are a people consecrated to the Lord your God: of all the peoples on earth the Lord your God chose you to be His treasured people. It is not because you are the most numerous of peoples that the Lord set His heart on you and chose you—indeed, you are the smallest of peoples; but it was because the Lord favored you and kept the oath He made to your fathers that the Lord freed you with a mighty hand and rescued you from the house of bondage, from the power of Pharaoh king of Egypt.

But for many Jews, this idea is controversial and uncomfortable. Notions of racial and genetic superiority have caused untold misery over the past century. Prayers like the one in our holiday liturgy that reads "thou has chosen us from among all other peoples, loved us, valued us, and exalted us above all nations," sound haughty, even arrogant, especially when read out of context. As a result, some Jews have abandoned the idea of chosenness, replacing uncomfortable prayers that make Jews sound superior and different with more politically correct universal prayers that offend no one.

What being chosen means, of course, is an entirely different matter. For persecuted Jews, like the Jews in Morocco at various times, the idea of chosenness allowed them to hold their heads high, even when their neighbors disdained them as accursed and inferior. It helped them survive oppression by fortifying them with the belief that

God's "treasured people" were destined to outlast their persecutors and someday be appropriately rewarded.

By contrast, modern Jews, living in countries like ours that preach equality, have more often described chosenness as a responsibility and obligation. Growing up, I often heard rabbis preach that, as a chosen people, we have a special "mission unto the nations" requiring us to uphold monotheism, live exemplary lives, and promote social justice. The Jewish philosopher Martin Buber warned that "if you boast of being chosen instead of living up to it, if you turn election into a static object instead of obeying it as a command, you forfeit it."

Now that I have studied other religions and peoples, I recognize that there is nothing unique about the Jewish conception of chosenness. Lots of nations from ancient times to the present have put forth similar ideas. Even now, I know Christians who are persuaded that they have superseded the Jews as God's chosen people, and Muslims who are no less certain that the true elect of God are Muslim. The British, for years, believed that they were the chosen people; so too did the French, the Germans, the Russians, the Afrikaners in South Africa, and even the Swedes. As for Americans, the idea that our country is "God's new Israel" began with the Puritans and still finds many devoted adherents today.

But that does not mean that chosenness and distinctiveness are bad ideas that Jews and others should abandon. Perhaps it is a good thing that every nation and faith believes that it is God's own special treasure! Historically, indeed, visions of chosenness have served both noble and ignoble purposes, promoting persecution of the "unchosen," as well as selfless efforts to make ours a better world. When a "chosen people" conceives of itself as a "master race" and attempts to put down those it disdains, that is a disaster—as we Jews know all too well from our experience with Nazism. But when a "chosen people" labors to elevate itself, to create a distinctive and "great society" serving as a beacon to others—then, it seems to me, chosenness is a godsend, a marvelous benefit not only for one people but for humanity at large.

Once upon a time, Maimuna brought together Morocco's "chosen people." Today, this celebration reminds us how culturally diverse our people is. Food, family, and a sense of distinctiveness maintain the present-day Moroccan Jewish community, even here in the United States. But who knows for how long?

I hope that I am invited back to Maimuna next year; maybe you can join me. For now, though, I am off to Jerusalem. I will be sure to write to you from there.

Love,
Abba

3

REMEMBERING THE HOLOCAUST

Yom ha-Shoah

Dear Leah,

I'm writing to you from Jerusalem, where a few hours ago, precisely at 10 A.M., the air raid sirens sounded. I was panicked, imagining the worst. I expected everyone to start running for shelter. But instead, an astonishing thing happened. Everyone around me stood stark still. The joggers on the street froze. Walkers stopped in their tracks. Automobiles braked to a halt, and some people got out and stood at attention. An older woman on the sidewalk wept quietly. For two full minutes, only the sound of the sirens filled the air: nobody spoke and no radios broke the spell (the sirens sounded on the radio too). I watched the scene, and I too remembered: Today is Yom ha-Shoah, Holocaust Remembrance Day.

Yom ha-Shoah falls on the twenty-seventh day of the Hebrew month of Nisan. In 1951, Israel's very first Knesset (its parliament) established that date. They carefully set it between the end of Passover and Israel

Independence Day, so that it coincides with the mid-point of the monthlong Warsaw Ghetto uprising but does not conflict with other holidays. The date also serves as an annual reminder that the slaughter of six million Jews immediately preceded the State of Israel's birth.

Some Jewish leaders opposed having a special day to commemorate the Holocaust. The Jewish calendar hardly lacks for the remembrance of tragedies, they pointed out. To their mind, the Holocaust differed from previous persecutions only in degree but was rooted in the same age-old hatred. They proposed instead to add Holocaust themes to an existing memorial day: either the major fast day of the Ninth of Av (Tishah be-Av) in summer, when so many other Jewish tragedies are recalled, or the half-forgotten minor fast day of the Tenth of Tevet, in winter, commemorating the start of the siege of Jerusalem by Babylon's King Nebuchadnezzar more than twenty-five hundred years ago.

But others insisted that the Holocaust was a unique event, different in both degree and kind from the persecutions, expulsions, and pogroms that Jews had known throughout their tumultuous history. Linking the memorial to an existing fast day, they felt, would dishonor the six million who perished. They feared that it would undermine the Holocaust's distinctiveness and insult the memory of the many non-religious Jews who died. Those Jews may not have fasted or believed in God, but they faced the same gas chambers and crematoria as those who were more observant.

Ultimately, in good Jewish fashion, both sides won. Religious Jews continue to recall the Holocaust on days like the Ninth of Av and the Tenth of Tevet (and in Sabba's case, on Passover as well), but the "official" day set aside for Holocaust remembrance in Israel—and now in the United States and Canada as well—became Yom ha-Shoah. Just to make things more complicated, the United Nations, in 2005, set aside January 27 as the International Day of Commemoration in Memory of the Victims of the Holocaust, commemorating the day that Auschwitz-Birkenau, the largest Nazi death camp, was liberated by the Soviet army in 1945. Several European countries have now adopted that date as International Holocaust Remembrance Day.

Here in Jerusalem, Yom ha-Shoah is a somber day, with special programming on radio and TV, commemorations in schools, and solemn ceremonies throughout the city. In the past, Holocaust survivors played a central role in these commemorations, bearing witness through their stories to the unbearable conditions in the ghettos, the gruesomeness of the death camps, and the cold-bloodedness of the many local mass murders in which so many Jews perished. But now, with the passage of time, the number of Holocaust survivors who can actually participate in Yom ha-Shoah observances is dwindling. Every year there are fewer of them. In a decade or two, the very last eyewitnesses to the Holocaust will be dead.

To me, this is a frightening prospect. How then will the Holocaust be remembered? Will it be remembered at all?

Back when Ima and I were children, nobody could possibly have questioned whether the Holocaust happened. We saw people with numbers tattooed on their arms and quickly came to understand that they had lived through the concentration camps. Many of those without physical marks, we found out, were touched by the Holocaust too. Some of them personally experienced *Kristallnacht* (The Night of Broken Glass), November 9–10, 1938, when attacks against Jews reverberated throughout Germany. One who was there once described to me how synagogues were destroyed, stores looted, homes destroyed, and thousands of Jewish men rounded up and taken off to concentration camps—a prelude of horrors yet to come.

Some of the parents of our friends growing up suffered greatly while fleeing the Nazis. They lost their homes, their worldly possessions, and their communities. Many recalled parents and other close relatives who disappeared, never to be heard from again. "Mrs. Levy lost two children in Europe," Sabba once explained, when I pointed to a neighbor who always looked teary-eyed whenever she saw us in the street. Another neighbor had lost practically his entire family in Europe, yet loved playing with young Jewish children like us. Each Jewish child, he declared, represented one more victory over Hitler.

You might not realize it, but yours will be the very last generation of Jews able to say that you actually knew survivors of the Holocaust. That's why it is so important that your school bring a survivor to speak about her experiences, and why it was so important to me that you come to know our older extended family members, Larry and Michael, who suffered unbearably in the concentration camps but managed to rebuild their lives in the United States. Decades from now, when your future grandchildren ask you questions, you will still be able to bear witness. You will be able to report hearing the story of the Holocaust directly from those who personally lived through it.

You should keep in mind that Jews were not the only victims of the Nazis—some of my students made this point forcefully to me a few years ago. The Gypsy (Romani) people, homosexuals, the handicapped, Communists, and anyone deemed an opponent of the German Reich, the state, also were targeted. Indeed, millions of non-Jews perished in World War II—a fact that we must never forget.

But it is also critical to remember that Jews were attacked with special vehemence—so much so that Nazi

Germany deemed even non-Jewish descendants of Jews to be Jewish by "race" and murdered them. Therein lies the uniqueness of the Holocaust from our perspective: It entailed nothing less than a worldwide war against the Jewish people. The poet Abba Kovner, who fought against the Nazis in Vilna and later settled in Israel, expressed this movingly in words that I try to reread each year at this time:

> *For the first time*
>
> *a whole nation was consigned to destruction by order of a government, which organized, planned to the last detail, practiced, and carried out a giant safari, and the hunt was maintained summer and winter, from the Atlantic coast to the foothills of the Caucasus, from the frozen North sea to the shores of the Mediterranean, everywhere, with no pause for holidays, day and night, in*
>
> *the high noon of the twentieth century;*
>
> *and assistants of every tongue took part, in every land, by agreement and on one condition, that the hunted be members of the Jewish people, men and women, young and old, pregnant, sick, disabled, and healthy, with no exceptions, and to this one purpose were allotted all the financial resources, the transport and the communication services required;*

*and the hunt for Jews continued as planned for almost
a hundred thousand hours, which is twelve years,
three months, and fifty days without end;*

and the Jewish people had no shield or savior.

No asylum, no escape.

We know, of course, that some Jews did escape—
usually with little more than the clothes on their backs.
But far more did not. Most of the nations of the world,
including, I am sorry to say, the United States and
Canada, stringently limited the number of Jews permitted to enter their countries. With antisemitism rising and
economic conditions still depressed, two-thirds of Americans in 1938 believed that Jewish refugees should be
kept out of the country. In 1939, Congress and the president doomed a bill to admit twenty-thousand refugee
children into the United States. When it came to issuing
visas to refugees, American government officials pursued
a policy of postponement after postponement. Nor were
other countries any better. In March 1938, thirty-two
countries met to discuss ways of saving Jews but came up
with no solutions. England refused to admit more Jews
into Palestine. Latin American nations admitted some
Jews but then barred their doors. Cuba actually revoked
the entry permits of many Jews. Almost a thousand Jews
sailed to Cuba on the passenger ship *St. Louis* in 1939,

believing that they would find refuge there, but found themselves barred; nor would America or any Caribbean country admit them. Eventually, the boat sailed back to Europe, where most of its passengers perished.

Had the State of Israel existed at that time, perhaps this whole story would have ended differently. Certainly, Jewish refugees would have had a place to go. But since nobody at that time seemed to want the Jews, Adolf Hitler felt emboldened to exterminate them. By early 1942, he and his close associates were discussing a "final solution" to the Jewish problem—meaning mass murder. Meeting at Wannsee, in a lakeside neighborhood of Berlin, they spelled out the plan to the heads of Germany's main ministries. Within months, a series of extermination camps were created at Sobibor, Treblinka, Majdanek, and Auschwitz—those terrible places you've probably heard of—to speed the process through the use of poison gas.

In Russia, which Germany attacked in 1941, special German task forces known as *Einsatzgruppen* targeted Jews, mowing them down with machine guns until they all lay dead. Sometimes they used gas vans to annihilate their victims. Sabba, as you know, had a photograph of the gas vans used to murder the Jews of his father's hometown. Many times, Nazi troops and sympathizers gathered entire populations, had them dig their own graves, and shot them dead on the spot. In Babi Yar, not far from Kiev, during a period of less than forty-eight hours, 33,000 Jews were robbed of all valuables, stripped, lined up by a ravine, and shot so they would fall into it. Most of the Jews of Greece—an ancient community and home to a large enclave of Sephardic Jews who had come from Spain and Portugal—were deported to Auschwitz in spring 1943 and never returned. A year later, some 437,000 Jews from Hungary were deported to Auschwitz in the space of just two months. Most of them were murdered too.

You asked me once why more Jews did not resist. Zdeněk Ornest, a teenager locked away in the concentration camp in Terezin, asked the same question in the very midst of the Holocaust. Writing in the secret boys' magazine, *Vedem*, produced in the camp, he described a group punishment meted out in 1943 against the entire camp population, which was forced to stand at attention outside in the cold for twelve long hours:

> *There were 30,000 of us and only a few of them, yet there was nothing we could do in our impotence. It was not enough to call out, "Hurrah, up and at them!" as one would in a revolution. We had no weapons and they would have gunned us down. We were all very weak as well.*

Despite their weakness, many Jews did try to resist. For some, that meant spiritual resistance: practicing Judaism in the face of the Nazi onslaught and educating their children under cramped ghetto conditions in defiance of the Nazi ban. Others fought back by courageously escaping: jumping from moving trains, digging under fences, and then making their way, sometimes over long distances and on foot, in search of freedom. For still others, resistance meant battling to remain alive; adamantly refusing to give up hope; struggling with every ounce of strength and determination against cold, hunger, disease, hard labor, and despair.

Resistance, in some cases, also meant taking up arms. Individual Jews escaped into the forest to fight as partisans against the Nazis. They gathered weapons within the ghettos to use when there were no other options, as in the Warsaw Ghetto uprising that I wrote to you about just before Passover. They participated in over twenty-three other uprisings against the Nazis in ghettos, labor camps, and death camps. A few courageous Jews even managed to set fire to a crematorium at the death camp of Auschwitz-Birkenau.

Taken together, these acts of resistance help to explain how some three million Jews survived in Europe when the war ended, despite the Nazis' best efforts to exterminate them. But by then, at least six million other Jews—two-thirds of European Jewry—lay dead.

Where was God when all of this was going on? Perhaps, as some theologians claim, God was hiding. Perhaps, as others insist, God was weeping. Perhaps the mystery is so great that it transcends our ability to comprehend it. But if we wonder how Jews can continue to believe in God after the Holocaust, surely we must wonder even more how Jews can continue to believe in humanity! Astonishingly, an inscription found on the walls of a cellar in Cologne, Germany, where Jews hid from the Nazis, suggests that even in the very midst of darkness, some Jews did continue to believe:

> *I believe in the sun even when it is not shining.*
> *I believe in love even when feeling it not.*
> *I believe in God even when He is silent.*

Can we do less?

A GROUP OF YOUNG PEOPLE here privately admitted to me last week that they were tired of hearing about the Holocaust. "It's coming out of our ears," they complained. "Can't we change the subject?" I've heard similar laments from kids back home, some of whom speak of experiencing "Holocaust fatigue." Mind you, these are not the vicious lunatics who deny that the Holocaust happened or the demagogues who maintain that Jews invented the story for some nefarious purpose. Those kinds of cranks, conspiracy theorists, and hate-mongers have long existed and are generally not worth our time. These young people are normal kids suffering from an overdose of Holocaust education. The central fact that they know about Jews is that the Nazis sought to destroy them. Years of learning about the Holocaust in school, reading about the Holocaust in books, listening to Holocaust lectures, viewing Holocaust films, traipsing through Holocaust museums, and trudging to Holocaust sites overseas have taken their toll. What they call "Holocaust fatigue" is a result of their knowing more about six years of Jewish tragedy than about three thousand years of Jewish creativity.

Widespread abuse of Holocaust imagery only exacerbates this problem. When every evil in the world is labeled a "Holocaust"—abortion, mistreatment of animals, slavery, the plight of Palestinians in Gaza, and more—then the very word Holocaust loses its meaning. No wonder some young people no longer want to hear about it!

The question is how to help everyone find the right balance. Just as Yom ha-Shoah is but one day in the Jewish calendar, so the Nazi Holocaust, it seems to me, needs to be contextualized within a broad understanding of Jewish history and achievement. Although we dare not forget the Holocaust and must ponder its lessons, we also dare not undermine the Holocaust through inappropriate analogies and obsessive fixations.

I would love to know your thoughts about this. I have always had a sense, in your case, that Holocaust awareness made you a more socially conscious person. News stories about ethnic cleansing in Bosnia, genocide in Rwanda, and mass murders in Darfur affected you as deeply as they did because you saw parallels between what was going on in those far-off places and what the

Nazis had done to our people. You learned important lessons from the Holocaust about your responsibilities to persecuted men, women, and children around the world. Without forgetting the particular impact that the Holocaust had on Jews, you nevertheless were sensitized by your study of the Holocaust to the suffering of oppressed people everywhere. That is the kind of balance that I hope we can impart to young people in the years ahead. We need to remember the Holocaust, learn appropriate lessons from it, and be inspired by those tragic events to shape a better tomorrow.

As I WRITE THESE WORDS, Yom ha-Shoah is coming to an end here in Jerusalem. Soon dusk will fall, regular TV and radio shows will resume, and life will return to its normal pace. No shofar will sound to mark the closing of the day, as it does on Yom Kippur, nor will the day end, as the Sabbath does, with *Havdalah*, the ceremony marking the passage from sacred time to ordinary time. So, for lack of an official ritual, I chant to myself the last verses of *Megilat ha-Shoah*, the Shoah Scroll, written not long ago by a child of Holocaust survivors, Avigdor Shinan. To me, its words capture the enduring message of this day for your generation and generations to come:

> *Do not mourn too much, but do not sink into the forgetfulness of apathy.*

Do not allow days of darkness to return; weep, but
wipe the tears away.
Do not absolve and do not exonerate; do not attempt
to understand.
Learn to live without an answer. . . .
Live!

Hope to see you soon!

Love,
Abba

4

CELEBRATING ISRAEL

Yom ha-Atsma'ut

Dear Leah,

I am back in Boston today, but all morning I've been thinking about my first trip to Israel, in 1965. Israel was a small, third world country in those days. Plumbing was primitive, telephones were scarce, and good-quality meat was almost nonexistent. Eggplant, rye bread, and watermelon were the staple foods. Poverty lined the faces of beggars and street peddlers. Rickety, fume-belching buses and large taxicabs dominated the roads; private cars were pretty rare. In some cities, farm animals roamed freely. Traveling from one place to another inevitably made me carsick. Even the trip up from Tel Aviv to Jerusalem required long hours of travel along a narrow winding road. When I finally arrived, I found that Jerusalem more closely resembled a large town than a capital city. Although home to one hundred and eighty thousand Jews, the city's dominant feature was the Mandelbaum Gate, the boundary separating Israeli Jerusalem from the Jordanian sector. Danger signs warned pedestrians to keep away from the no-man's-land and disputed areas. Jordanian soldiers, their guns trained on the Israelis, stood in plain sight.

I conjure up these dim memories today because it is Yom ha-Atsma'ut, Israel Independence Day. Having visited Israel for the first time when the country was but seventeen years old, I appreciate more than do most people how much it has grown and changed over time. News stories focus largely on Israel's never-ending battles with its Arab neighbors, but I know that there is much more to the country than that.

Israelis actually spent yesterday, the day *prior* to Yom ha-Atsma'ut, thinking about the thousands of men, women, and children who sacrificed their lives for the state. Yom ha-Zikkaron, Israel's Day of Remembrance, is roughly akin to our Memorial Day, except that everyone in Israel seems to have a relative or friend whose death from war or terrorism they recall. Rather than being a day of sales at the malls, it is a day for visiting the graves of fallen loved ones.

Sabba used to remember his friend Esther—newly arrived from England, young, idealistic, full of life—who fell in the War of Independence; she was in her early twenties. I, of course, remember Aaron: handsome, ambitious, newly married, and awaiting his first child. He was incinerated in his tank on the opening day of yet another war.

Many of those killed in Israel's wars were about your age. I shudder when I see their photographs on the walls of friends and relatives in Israel. They look like such promising young people, so much, frankly, like you and your friends. But "they sacrificed their lives for the sanctity of the Divine name, for their people, and for their land," as the traditional memorial prayer puts it. Esther, Aaron, and so many others died prematurely, so that the State of Israel might continue to live.

And live it has. During my visit to Israel a few weeks ago, I was struck by how much had changed since 1965. Today, Israel is a first-world country, where almost everybody sports a cell phone (in fact, the first cell phone was invented there), and more than two hundred thousand people work in high-tech fields (instant messaging and the Intel pentium processor were also Israeli inventions). Luxurious accommodations abound, many featuring air-conditioning, cable television, whirlpool baths, and even deluxe spas. Excellent restaurants and giant groceries overflow with high-quality foods of every sort, meat included. A new bus lane speeds the way for modern buses and sleek taxis, while most people drive cars—late model ones—and they tend to drive them recklessly. Everywhere, new roads, some with elaborate tunnels, have reduced driving times appreciably. The trip up from Tel Aviv to Jerusalem now takes less than an hour on a multi-lane highway, while Israel's first limited-access toll road has cut driving times to the north even further. As for

Jerusalem, its population has ballooned to include six hundred and seventy-five thousand Jews, making it the third-largest Jewish community in the world, after Tel Aviv and New York. In place of the ugly boundary that once disfigured the very heart of the city, neighborhoods filled with beautiful houses stand proud.

For all that is new and modern about Israel, its greatest allure, for me, is the country's fascinating antiquity. Everywhere one looks, one sees sites mentioned in the Bible. Thanks to archaeological finds, I can, with help from a guide, actually envisage where and how our ancestors lived in times past: in the days of the patriarchs and matriarchs more than three thousand years ago; during the era of the Judges and the monarchy of King Saul (1200–1000 BCE); during the years when King David and King Solomon ruled over a united kingdom (1004–928 BCE); at the time of the magnificent Second Temple built by King Herod about the year 19 BCE and destroyed by the Romans in the year 70 CE; and during all the post-Temple centuries. Never since those days was the land of Israel totally barren of Jews. Always—when the land was occupied by the Romans and most Jews were exiled, when the remaining Jews in Palestine (as its conquerors dubbed it) were cruelly persecuted, when the land was conquered by Arabs in 638, by crusaders in 1099, by Saladin in 1187, by the Turks in 1516, and by the British in 1917, even when no one could find work and food was scarce—tenacious Jews insisted upon staying put in their ancestral homeland. Imagine, over three thousand years of continuous Jewish presence in the Land of Israel. It is, as my students like to say, a mind-blowing concept.

Of course, for almost nineteen hundred years, Jews in the land of Israel lived under subjugation, ruled successively by Romans, Byzantines, Persians, Arabs, crusaders, Mamluks, Ottoman Turks, and Englishmen. Jews around the world prayed for a return to Zion, but the vast majority of them continued to live, as we do, in the diaspora.

The modern call to return to Zion arose, in large measure, in response to two important movements that captured widespread attention in the late nineteenth century: antisemitism and nationalism. People like your great-grandparents and great-great-grandparents in Eastern Europe found themselves reviled as religious and cultural outsiders in their own home countries. Anti-Jewish violence and persecutions abounded: riots; pogroms; false accusations; restrictions on education; and limits on where Jews could live, work, and travel. In response, many Jews sought to find new and safer homes abroad. They were about three times as likely to leave home as their Eastern European neighbors, many of whom, for economic reasons, were also on the move. But where could all those Jews go? And what guarantee was there that they would not meet with similar persecutions again?

For a few decades, Western European and New World countries, particularly the United States, welcomed Jewish immigrants, but by World War I those gates had mostly shut tight. There remained, many felt, only one solution: a Jewish homeland, a place where Jews could finally be welcomed as "insiders" and live safely, in control of their own destiny. Since Jews' historic home in the land of Israel was significantly underpopulated—only about half a million Muslims, Christians, and Jews lived there late into the nineteenth century—that seemed like the natural location. When Great Britain captured the land of Israel from the Turks in 1917, Britain promised to make it available to Jews. The well-known Balfour Declaration made that promise explicit:

> *His Majesty's Government view with favour the establishment in Palestine of a national home for the Jewish people, and will use their best endeavours to facilitate the achievement of this object.*

Looking back, of course, that was much easier said than done. The Arabs had other ideas, the British prevaricated, and terrorist violence aimed at preventing the establishment of a "national home for the Jewish people" led to many deaths. Then in the 1930s and 1940s, when so many of our relatives were attempting to flee Hitler and found every country's gates shut tight against them, the need for a Jewish homeland became more and more apparent. "Home," the poet Robert Frost once observed, "is the place where, when you have to go there, they have to take you in." Never did Jews need a home so badly and suffer its absence so acutely as during the Holocaust. Millions, including some of our own relatives, might have been saved, had a Jewish homeland existed before World War II. Better late than never, the State of Israel was born three years after the war ended, on May 14, 1948, the fifth of Iyar, according to the Jewish calendar.

Sabba heard the news live on a shortwave radio in London and once described the scene to me. It took place on a Friday afternoon, just prior to the Sabbath. A few hours earlier, the British, who had governed the country since World War I, had pulled down their Union Jack and prepared to return home. Now, according to the United Nations, the land was to be partitioned between Jews and Arabs; each was to have a state of its own. This was the moment that leaders of the Jewish community in Palestine, led by David Ben-Gurion, later Israel's first prime minister, had been waiting for. At the Tel Aviv Museum, with crowds surging below them, Ben-Gurion banged down his gavel, while the crowd began singing *Hatikva*—the Zionist anthem meaning "hope." Then, in carefully measured Hebrew, Ben-Gurion read out the Declaration of Independence that brought the State of Israel into existence:

> *We, the members of the National Council . . . by the virtue of the natural and historic right of the Jewish people and of the resolution of the General Assembly of*

the United Nations, hereby proclaim the establishment
of a Jewish State in Palestine, to be called Israel.

The declaration, which is as important to Israelis as the 1776 Declaration of Independence is to Americans, began with a ringing affirmation of history, dating the Jewish presence in the land of Israel back to the Bible. Even after "being forcibly exiled from their land," it declared, "the Jewish people remained faithful to it in all the countries of their dispersion, never ceasing to pray and hope for their return and the restoration of their national freedom." Committing itself to humanitarian values, the declaration promised Israel's Arab citizens "full and equal citizenship." It asked neighboring countries to cooperate in helping to advance the "peaceful progress and development of the Middle East." Most important of all, it set forth the basic rights of all of Israel's inhabitants, Jews and non-Jews alike:

THE STATE OF ISRAEL will be open to the immigration
of Jews from all countries of their dispersion; will
promote the development of the country for the benefit
of all its inhabitants; will be based on the precepts of
liberty, justice and peace taught by the Hebrew
Prophets; will uphold the full social and political
equality of all its citizens, without distinction of race,
creed or sex; will guarantee full freedom of conscience,

worship, education and culture; will safeguard the sanctity and inviolability of the shrines and Holy Places of all religions; and will dedicate itself to the principles of the Charter of the United Nations.

I've often wondered what would have happened had Israel's neighbors welcomed the establishment of the tiny new state instead of vowing to crush it. Think of all the lives that would have been spared! Imagine all the good that might have been accomplished had the billions of dollars spent on weaponry been devoted instead to fighting poverty and disease, to promoting education and housing and employment. But instead, within twenty-four hours of declaring its independence, Israel was fighting for its life. Bombs fell on Tel Aviv, the eighty-five thousand Jews of Jerusalem were cut off and besieged, and armies from all the surrounding countries—Egypt, Jordan, Syria, Iraq, and Lebanon—invaded. "This will be a war of extermination," the secretary-general of the Arab League proclaimed, "a momentous massacre."

Israel won its independence after a bloody year-long war, but, sadly, its neighbors never made peace with its existence. Time and again—even now, some sixty years later—extremists talk of destroying the little state, driving its Jewish inhabitants into the sea, even of attacking it with nuclear weapons. Never in its entire existence has Israel enjoyed so much as one violence-free decade.

WHEN I WAS YOUNG, the people I knew looked upon tiny, embattled Israel as something of a heaven-on-earth. For all the dangers that it faced, it was, in our eyes, a kind of embryonic Jewish utopia, a safe spot for our people, a place where our fondest hopes and aims might be realized. We looked upon it as an extension of the American dream, a Jewish refuge where freedom, liberty, and social justice reigned supreme, an outpost of democracy that every American Jew could legitimately, proudly, and patriotically champion. Under Jewish leadership, we believed, Israel had made the desert bloom.

That, I know, is not the Israel that some people your age describe. They look upon Israel as an obstacle to peace, a country that persecutes Arabs, a theocracy governed by Orthodox Jews, a racist state, an apartheid state—some of them think that it is a state that should not exist at all. Supporting Israel is infinitely harder for your generation than it was for mine.

I vividly recall the June 1967 Six Day War when Israel's neighbors, without provocation, attempted to destroy the then-tiny Jewish state. You, by contrast, have witnessed decades of warfare, terrorism, counterterrorism, military occupation, and bloody resistance blamed on Israel's capture of Arab lands in June 1967. My generation felt confident that Israel was right and its Arabs neighbors were wrong in the Middle East conflict. Your generation asks many more questions and expresses many more doubts.

You will have to make up your own mind concerning Israel's policies, but I hope that you do so knowledgeably. Understand why a majority of the members of the United Nations voted to create a homeland for the Jewish people back in 1947. Learn about the millions of Jewish refugees from around the world, including hundreds of thousands of Jews expelled from Arab lands, who poured into Israel, and look how Israel turned those refugees into productive citizens. Compare the treatment of minorities in Israel and the treatment of minorities in neighboring states. Study Israel's democratic institutions and search for ones similar to them elsewhere in the Middle East. Read a reliable history of the Six Day War. Speak to Israel's victims of terror and see if you sympathize with their desire to do everything possible, including the building of high barriers, to prevent others from suffering the way they have.

In 1983 Bob Dylan made the case for Israel in a song called *Neighborhood Bully*. It made a great impression upon me when I heard it years ago, and now as you think about Israel, I recommend it to you at well. Amazing how little has changed in the generation since he wrote this!

> *Well, the neighborhood bully, he's just one man,*
> *His enemies say he's on their land.*
> *They got him outnumbered about a million to one,*
> *He got no place to escape to, no place to run.*
> *He's the neighborhood bully.*

The neighborhood bully just lives to survive,
He's criticized and condemned for being alive.
He's not supposed to fight back, he's supposed to have
*   thick skin,*
He's supposed to lay down and die when his door is
*   kicked in.*
He's the neighborhood bully.

The neighborhood bully been driven out of every land,
He's wandered the earth an exiled man.
Seen his family scattered, his people hounded and
*   torn,*
He's always on trial for just being born.
He's the neighborhood bully.

Well, he knocked out a lynch mob, he was criticized,
Old women condemned him, said he should apologize.
Then he destroyed a bomb factory, nobody was glad.
The bombs were meant for him.
He was supposed to feel bad.
He's the neighborhood bully.

Well, the chances are against it and the odds are slim
That he'll live by the rules that the world makes for
*   him,*
'Cause there's a noose at his neck and a gun at his
*   back,*
And a license to kill him is given out to every maniac.
He's the neighborhood bully.

You may wonder, once your mind is made up, whether you can both criticize Israel and love and support Israel, oppose the policies of Israel's government and join in the celebration of Yom ha-Atsma'ut? The answer, of course, is yes. Free people all over the world, Americans in particular, regularly criticize their country and love it as well. July Fourth celebrations in the United States and Bastille Day in France are scarcely confined just to supporters of the party in power at the moment! The same is true in Israel. Many Israelis, in my experience, both criticize their country and love it deeply.

What bothers me about some young people today, however, is that they have eyes only for Israel's shortcomings. Instead of celebrating Israel's creation and recognizing its accomplishments and aspirations, they mourn it as a "catastrophe," believing that the world would be better off without Jews having a homeland of their own. "The Zionist State known as 'Israel' is a regime that has no right to exist," screams a volume entitled *Israel: Opposing Viewpoints.* The motives of far too many of Israel's critics today—some of them self-styled "progressives" and some of them Jews—are not to see the world's only Jewish state improved but to see it destroyed. The fact that this might lead to the massacre of Israel's 5.5 million Jews, and deprive the rest of the world's Jews of a refuge, seems to leave them unmoved.

Israel, of course, can be legitimately criticized for its strategic failures, its mistreatment of its Arab citizens, its religious policies, and much more. Like most countries in the world, it has made many tragic mistakes. The key is learning how to distinguish legitimate criticisms of Israel from illegitimate ones. I take my cue from a quote I read from Thomas Friedman of the *New York Times*. "Criticizing Israel," he wrote, "is not anti-Semitic, and saying so is vile. But singling out Israel for opprobrium and international sanction—out of all proportion to any other party in the Middle East—is anti-Semitic, and not saying so is dishonest."

The Talmud declares, "He who reproves his neighbor with pure intent is worthy of a portion from God." Criticism, this implies, must be carefully evaluated: Much depends on the motives of the critic.

The unworthy critics today are easy to find. Their shrill voices are neither moderated by love nor tinged with sadness. Their desire is to see the Jewish state and its people destroyed.

The worthy critics, by contrast, are more scarce. Alive to the realities of contemporary Israel and the tragedies of the twentieth century, their words mingle praise along with reproof. They speak directly, sadly, and always in pain. They, in my experience, are the critics most worth heeding. They stimulate thought, debate, and action.

AMAZINGLY, given all the criticism that Israel receives, thousands of Jews from North America decide every year to settle there permanently. A few time their flights to be able to make *aliyah*, as moving to Israel is called, on Yom ha-Atsma'ut itself. Some are old and seek to live out their last days in Israel for religious reasons. There is an ancient belief that those who are buried in the land of Israel enjoy many privileges. But others arrive in their twenties and thirties, sometimes with young children in tow. As I understand it, they are drawn to Israel for ideological reasons. They feel that the beleaguered little country needs all the help it can get at this time, and they seek to put their skills to work on its behalf. In addition, many of them want to raise their children in a Jewish environment, where it is so much easier to keep kosher, observe Shabbat, and take off time for Jewish holidays. Personally, I am always glad to hear of North Americans settling in Israel. Over time, I hope, they will bring to the still-young Jewish state some of the values that we cherish and some of the lessons that we have learned about freedom.

Years ago, I happened to be in Israel for Yom ha-Atsma'ut, and I saw firsthand the street fairs, parades, air shows, religious services, outdoor barbecues, and grand fireworks that characterize the day. I remember watching the World Bible Contest, where young Jewish students from all over the world compete to answer questions concerning the Book of Books, and then I saw the ceremony that the government holds to mark its independence day, including the distribution of the "Israel Prize" to worthy citizens. Yom ha-Atsma'ut is the one day of the year when Israel celebrates itself.

For me here in America, though, Yom ha-Atsma'ut is usually a regular workday. Unless I make some special effort, like attending religious services or celebrating at the Jewish Community Center, the day passes unmarked and unnoticed. So now, I try to spend at least part of the day thinking about Israel: thinking about my relationship to the country and its people; thinking about my visits to Israel, the good times and the bad; and thinking about the Israel of my ideals, the Israel that I hope will one day be realized, if not in my lifetime, then perhaps in yours.

And then, when I am done thinking, I pray. I thank God for having established the State of Israel, the home now of 5.5 million Jews. I thank God for the miraculous rebirth of the Hebrew language and Hebrew culture. I thank God for the fact that there is now a Jewish homeland where Jews persecuted anywhere in the world can go and find refuge. And I thank God for protecting this small, vibrant state against mighty enemies who seek to wipe it off the face of the earth. Most of all, though, I pray for peace. Taking my cue from a new prayer for the State of Israel that I recently heard, I recite the following:

Cause Your spirit's influence to emanate upon all dwellers of our holy land. Remove from their midst hatred and enmity, jealousy and wickedness. Plant in

their hearts love and kinship, peace and friendship.
And soon fulfill the vision of Your prophet: "Nation
shall not lift up sword against nation. Let them learn
no longer ways of war."

Here's hoping!

Love,
Abba

5

TORAH

Shavuot

Dear Leah,

Last week, I read about a most extraordinary wedding. Hundreds of people showed up: Men sat on the right, women on the left. Beautiful bouquets festooned the sanctuary where the marriage took place. Periodically, everyone broke out in song. Some women keened lustily, emitting the throaty trills that Jewish women of Spanish heritage make on such occasions. The bride, all decked out in white, was actually carried into the ceremony. The groom, strange to relate, could not be seen at all. The marriage contract, written on parchment and beautifully illuminated, was duly unfurled, and read as follows:

> *On Friday, the sixth day of the month of Sivan . . .*
> *came before us the prince of princes and noble of nobles*
> *who is named Israel . . . and said to the dear and*
> *pleasant child of many qualities, the Torah, the perfect*

Law of God . . . be unto me as wife, thou who art
lovely as the moon, and I will betroth thee unto me for
ever. . . . And this bride, the holy Torah, was willing
and became his wife.

As you probably guessed, this was no ordinary wedding. Instead it was a ritual reenactment of the "marriage" between the people of Israel and the holy Torah. Annually, on the Jewish festival of Shavuot (meaning "weeks"), celebrated on the fiftieth day, or "Pentecost," after the second day of Passover, Jews with roots in the Eastern Mediterranean joyously solemnize this marriage. This is their way of commemorating the tradition that God gave the Torah to the children of Israel at Mount Sinai on that very day.

For the "wedding," the Torah was dressed up in white to resemble a bride. Like every Torah, it was written by hand in Hebrew on a parchment scroll by a religious scribe known as a *sofer*. It contains the first five books of the Bible (Genesis, Exodus, Leviticus, Numbers, Deuteronomy), called in English the "Pentateuch," or the "Five Books of Moses." Later in the service, the Torah was set down and opened, and, following the universal custom among Jews on Shavuot, the Ten Commandments were chanted from the book of Exodus. Then the whole story of what happened at Mount Sinai was recounted.

The word "Torah" embraces much more than the Ten Commandments, and more even than the Five Books of

Moses. The Hebrew word itself really means "teaching." Confusingly, Jews employ the word "Torah" in multiple senses, ranging from the narrowest meaning, the Torah scroll, to the "Oral Torah," the teachings of the rabbis, to the broadest meaning, which encompasses all Jewish teachings from the Bible to the present day. The holiday of Shavuot embraces each of these meanings. It commemorates the giving of the Torah, and it celebrates *all* of Jewish Torah: laws and lore, texts and interpretations of texts, the wisdom of ancient prophets and the wisdom of modern rabbis.

Together, these teachings form links in a great and unbroken chain of creative Torah scholarship reaching back (so some rabbis claimed) to a time even before the world was created and extending on indefinitely into the future. Jewish tradition holds that Moses received all the Torah at Mount Sinai and passed it on to his successor, Joshua, who then passed it on to his successors, and they to their successors, and so on, generation after generation, down to the present day. This tradition of the Torah being "passed on" should sound familiar to you. You have seen it reenacted in countless bar mitzvah and bat mitzvah ceremonies in which the scroll is conveyed from hand to hand, from grandparents to parents to children.

Did the Torah literally descend from heaven, passed along from God to Moses on Mount Sinai? That is for you to decide. For many Jews, past and present, this has been a fundamental belief, the very basis of their faith. By postulating that every syllable of the Bible reflects the unerring word of God, they can be confident that it represents nothing less than perfection and truth. Some even maintain that the Bible conceals hidden messages and codes.

Other Jews, though, have understood the idea of "Torah from Sinai" less literally. Even if they believe that the Torah is divinely given, they take what they call a more "critical" view, explaining repetitions and contradictions in the biblical text as reflections of different ancient oral traditions woven together by human hands. Some go further, insisting that the Torah was completely the work of human beings, produced by men and women who were highly creative and "divinely inspired."

The best thing to do is to study the Torah and come to your own conclusions. Treat yourself to a wide range of Jewish commentaries, ancient and modern, traditional and critical, and develop an approach to the text that works for you. This will take time, of course. Jewish tradition holds that the Torah has "seventy faces"—meaning almost limitless numbers of possible interpretations. "Just as a hammer shatters rock and generates numerous splinters," the Talmud, the great compilation of some five hundred years of ancient rabbinic wisdom, declares, "so may a single verse yield a multiplicity of meanings." To be properly understood, the Torah needs to be continually and conscientiously studied. Each reading, each rereading, each new commentary provides fresh insights and new layers of meaning.

Study, indeed, is how Jews have always shown respect for the Bible, the most widely read and most influential book of all time. A devoted student, whether traditional or modern, spends countless hours seeking, in Sabba's words, "to unfold the sense, meanings, purposes, intents, and applications of the biblical texts." The Shavuot "wedding" that I mentioned acknowledges this intensive and loving engagement with Torah. It compares it to a lifelong relationship with a partner.

I love this metaphor. To my mind, the kind of relationship that one has with the Torah, like any healthy relationship, leaves room for vigorous disputes, radical innovations, passion, anger, boredom, mischief, misbehavior, reconciliation, and above all maturation and growth. At the same time, it also demands careful tending. "Desert me for one day, and I will desert you for two," the ancient rabbis say in the Torah's name. Jews who take this admonition seriously study the Torah daily. The last thing they want is for their relationship with the Torah to grow cold and distant.

What happens if you do not take your relationship with the Torah so seriously? To be honest, you will be like most Jews—and, for that matter, most non-Jews. The average American, according to the pollsters, is a biblical illiterate. But since the Torah is almost universally seen as one of the Jewish people's greatest contributions to civilization, to be ignorant of it is (to say the least) rather embarrassing. Moreover, without at least some understanding of the Torah, Judaism is incomprehensible.

SHAVUOT IS MENTIONED in the Torah, but in ancient times the holiday had nothing whatsoever to do with Torah study. It was a pilgrimage festival tied in with the start of the harvest. Jews brought up the harvest's first fruits—the wheat, barley, grapes, figs, pomegranates, olive oil, and date honey for which ancient Israel was renowned—to the holy temple in Jerusalem as a thanksgiving offering to God. The Talmud details how the colorful ceremony was conducted, complete with rich ornamentation and flute playing. As people presented their offerings to the priest, they recited one of Judaism's most ancient prayers, affirming God's promise to the Jewish people, recalling past oppressions, and recapitulating Israel's history:

> I acknowledge this day before the Lord your God that I have entered the land that the Lord swore to our fathers to assign us. . . . My father was a fugitive Aramean. He went down to Egypt with meager numbers and sojourned there; but there he became a great and very populous nation. The Egyptians dealt harshly with us and oppressed us; they imposed heavy labor upon us. We cried to the Lord, the God of our fathers,

and the Lord heard our plea and saw our plight, our misery, and our oppression. The Lord freed us from Egypt by a mighty hand, by an outstretched arm and awesome power, and by signs and portents. He brought us to this place and gave us this land, a land flowing with milk and honey. Wherefore I now bring the first fruits of the soil which You, O Lord, have given me.

After the temple in Jerusalem was destroyed in the year 70, Judaism shifted away from agriculturally based festivals of this kind. Moreover, as Jews scattered to the far corners of the diaspora, the tradition of making three pilgrimages a year to Jerusalem became impractical. So, the rabbis reinterpreted Shavuot. From then on, the day became known as the anniversary of the giving of the Torah on Mount Sinai.

You learned, as a young child, one story concerning how the Torah was given. I remember your first-grade play, which made the point that the Torah was given exclusively to Jews. (The reenacted wedding between the Torah and Israel suggests the same thing.) In the play, based on an oft-repeated rabbinic legend, God initially offered the Torah to the other nations of antiquity; indeed, "there was not a nation at whose doors He did not knock." But because the Torah demanded such a high level of morality—no murder, no theft, no coveting, and so forth—each nation in turn rejected its teachings, until finally God turned to Israel. "All that the Lord has spoken we will do and obey," the people of Israel exclaimed together. (Remember how you and your classmates learned to shout out that line in Hebrew?) Because Israel alone accepted the Torah, it became, in the song that you all sang, "the heritage of the community of Jacob." Since then, God, Torah, and Israel have been inextricably interlinked.

By now, I hope you know that there are myriad Jewish legends concerning the giving of the Torah, and some of them disagree with the one that your class dramatized. An alternative story declares that the Torah *remains* God's gift to all the nations. That is why it was given "in the desert, publicly and openly, in a place belonging to no one." The goal was precisely to avoid making the Torah's teachings appear narrow, directed to Jews alone. Just as fire, water, and the desert "are free to all who come into the world," this tradition relates, "so also are the words of the Torah free to all who come into the world." No people has a monopoly on the Torah and its teachings.

Whichever story you prefer, this much is certain: for Jews, the Torah represents survival. Other nations perished when their countries were invaded and their temples destroyed, but thanks to the Torah, Judaism became a portable faith—one that Jews could literally carry with them from place to place. When the Temple in Jerusalem was destroyed two thousand years ago, a far-sighted rabbi named Johanan Ben Zakkai established a center for Torah study in the small coastal city of Jabneh, and Jewish learning was maintained. That same story has been repeated time and again in our history: Jews expelled from one place bring their Torah to a new one. So long as the Torah survives, Jews survive.

WOMEN HAVE HISTORICALLY played an enormous role in Jewish survival, and the Bible makes clear that women as well as men received the Torah at Mount Sinai. Study, the Bible plainly declares, is for everyone: "Gather the people—men, women, children, and the strangers in your communities—that they may hear and so learn to revere the Lord your God and to observe faithfully every word of this Torah." Note that no intermediary stands between the individual and the teachings of Judaism. Every man, woman, and child enjoys direct, personal access to Judaism's sacred books.

This democratization of Jewish learning—the fact that men and women from all walks of life can study Torah, not just rabbis and scholars—is, to my mind, one of Judaism's most appealing and distinctive features. For centuries, ordinary citizens spent two months a year learning during what were called *yarḥe kallah*, month-long assemblies, a forerunner of today's adult education courses. Later, study circles devoted to one or another Jewish text became common among Jews. Men, as well as some women, would gather to study the Bible, the Talmud, or *Ein Ya'akov*, a treasury of ethical and inspirational teachings of the rabbis. A popular sixteenth-century Yiddish text encouraged everyone, including the most ignorant Jew, to fix a time for the study of Torah each and every day. Even a brief period of daily study was acceptable, the author explained, so long as the time set aside was uninterrupted, and business was forced to wait.

In real life, however, Torah study remained, for centuries, largely the preserve of men. "He who teaches his daughter Torah is considered as if he taught her licentiousness," the Talmud proclaims in one place, and Moses Maimonides, in his great medieval law code, exempted women from Torah study since "most women's minds are not properly directed to being taught." Your own grandmother, raised before World War II in a fervently Orthodox home, never so much as studied Hebrew. She only learned it later, after she was married. The vast majority of Jewish women (notwithstanding a few famous exceptions) never studied the sources of Judaism in the original. Most of what they knew they learned from their parents or from popular books written especially for women.

Fortunately, times have changed. Today, in most parts of the Jewish world, women study Torah on a par with men. "Not only is it *permitted* to teach Torah and reverence towards God to the daughters of our generation, but there is an *absolute duty* to do so," a leading twentieth-century Orthodox rabbi decreed. Even the Talmud, which few women studied when I was growing up, has now become part of your Jewish education. Indeed, both in America and in Israel, there are schools where women can pursue Jewish learning at the most advanced levels. As a result, hundreds of non-Orthodox Jewish women have been ordained as rabbis in their movements in recent years, and tens of thousands of women from across the spectrum of Jewish life have become learned Jews who can read and teach Jewish sources in the original.

The possibilities for Jewish learning have been further broadened by two remarkable developments in recent years. First, new printing technologies have made it possible to publish traditional Jewish texts inexpensively. Some may now even be printed for free from the Internet. This has served to further democratize Jewish learning. Even the poor can enjoy broad access to many of the great books of Jewish tradition. Second, a substantial number of traditional Jewish sources have been translated. Those unlearned in Hebrew and Aramaic now can study Judaism's greatest books in a language they can understand. Practically every major Jewish text, including the Talmud, can be mastered in translation.

Shavuot provides a great opportunity to celebrate this broadening of Jewish learning by delving into one or another Jewish text. Indeed, there is a custom, on the first evening of the holiday, to study all night long! In my community, men as well as women listen to lectures, study texts on their own or with a partner, intone morning prayers by the first rays of the sun, and only then go to sleep. It is an unforgettable experience.

This custom of staying up all night to study on the eve of Shavuot was established more than four hundred years ago (equivalent to the day before yesterday, in Jewish time) by mystical Jews in Israel's holy city of Safed. One of them, Solomon Alkabetz, author of that Sabbath evening prayer that you like to sing, Lecha Dodi, reported that precisely at midnight, he and his learned companion, Joseph Karo, heard a divine voice calling out to them from amid their scholarly devotions. "By denying yourself sleep," the voice declared, "you have ascended . . . far on high. . . . Cease not from studying." Hoping to hear this "exceedingly pleasant voice" again, other mystics joined them in late-night study on the first night of Shavuot, and the practice soon spread far and wide throughout the Jewish world—perhaps stimulated by the arrival of coffee, at approximately the same time, in many communities where Jews then lived. Before long, a liturgy for the all-night study session had been developed, and the practice acquired a name: Tikkun Leil Shavuot, the order of study for Shavuot eve.

Today, I do not know anybody who has ever heard the divine voice at midnight on the first night of Shavuot. But I do know lots of people who stay up late to study. Some follow the prescribed ritual: an anthology that includes the opening and closing verses of every Torah portion, of every book of the entire Bible, and of various rabbinic and mystical works. By slogging through the beginning and ending lines of so many books, those who follow this practice symbolically embrace a wide range of traditional Jewish writings, the "length and breadth" of the Torah.

More commonly, people study anything Jewish that strikes their fancy during the long night—a biblical book, a chapter from the Talmud, a mystical work, a philosophical treatise, a law code, a commentary, a volume of rabbinic questions and answers, or perhaps some engaging piece of esoterica. Well-populated Jewish communities sometimes post long lists of nighttime lectures—a veritable Shavuot teach-in—broken up by periodic refreshments. Since custom holds that dairy foods are preferred on the first day of Shavuot, a favorite delicacy is cheesecake.

CHEESECAKE AND LOVE OF TORAH may unite Jews on Shavuot, but a hard question remains: Must one also *follow* all of Judaism's teachings, or may one be selective, ignoring, for example, those Torah teachings that run counter to science, conscience, or contemporary culture? Must one accept every word of the Torah literally?

Sorry, but there is no single, easy answer to these questions. You will not be surprised to learn that different rabbis and different Jewish movements have vehemently disagreed over precisely these issues. There are restrictive views and permissive ones, liberal views and conservative ones. Jews have continually debated what the Torah says and means, some rabbis creatively reinterpreting its words to meet new challenges, others taking a more "strict constructionist" approach. The justices of U.S. Supreme Court carry on similar debates concerning how to interpret the American Constitution. Your job, building upon those who have come before you, is to study, think, and develop your own approach to these questions. In doing so, you will define what kind of Jew you are, how you relate to other Jews, and how you relate to the world at large.

"Why not just focus on the Ten Commandments?" a student once asked me. "Everybody believes in them." We read them aloud from the Torah on the holiday of Shavuot, and they are frequently (some claim *too* frequently) displayed on government property. "They are the central laws that Jews share with their neighbors," the student declared. "They form the basis for both Jewish law and American law. There is no conflict about them at all."

I had a chance to think about this recently when I examined the famous Ten Commandments monument at the Texas State Capitol. Some wanted that monument removed, arguing that it violated America's separation of church and state, but the U.S. Supreme Court voted to let it stand, based on "the role played by the Ten Commandments in our Nation's heritage."

What surprised me, when I actually looked at the monument, was how different the text of the Ten Commandments displayed there reads from the one that we Jews learn about in our tradition and read aloud from the Torah on Shavuot. Of course, our text has the great virtue of being in the original Hebrew. But even the accompanying English translation diverges significantly from what appears on the monument. It turns out that there is more conflict concerning the Ten Commandments than even I had realized.

For one thing, we Jews actually speak of ten divine statements—*dibrot* in Hebrew—not ten commandments, which would be *mitzvot*. Indeed, there are as many as thirteen individual commandments scattered among the ten "statements."

More significantly, we Jews number the statements differently from the way the monument does. "I am the Lord," in our tradition, wins pride of place as the opening "commandment." Some Jewish commentators insist that everything follows from that critical first one. "Thou shall have no other gods before Me," which the monument places first, is therefore number two in our books. Likewise, the monument opens two different commandments with the phrase "Thou shalt not covet." Our tradition combines those two into one.

Most important of all, our *understanding* of some of the commandments differs from that found on the monument. For example, the monument declares, "Thou shalt not *kill*." Our translation (rooted, I have to boast, in the original Hebrew), reads, "Thou shalt not *murder.*" Murder and kill mean very different things as a matter of law, and they carry altogether different implications.

The Sabbath, too, looks different in our Bible from the text on the monument. The latter reads, "Remember the Sabbath Day to keep it holy," but never defines when the Sabbath occurs, what keeping the Sabbath holy means, or why God established the Sabbath in the first place. Our text devotes fully fifty-five Hebrew words (ninety-two in English translation) to the Sabbath, spelling out precisely that it falls on "the seventh day," that work is forbidden, and that it recalls the seventh day of creation, when God rested. That is why we Jews observe the Sabbath on Saturday, not Sunday, and why observant Jews are so careful to avoid work of any kind on that day.

Admittedly, the monument and our Jewish text do share numerous elements in common. Both, for example, mandate the honoring of father and mother. And both, in almost identical terms, prohibit adultery, stealing, and bearing false witness. But the differences between the monument's Ten Commandments and the Ten Divine Statements that Jews read on Shavuot demonstrate that the Ten Commandments are a lot less universal than generally imagined. Not only do Jews and non-Jews read, number, translate, and understand the Ten Commandments in disparate ways, but in general we Jews maintain our own distinct understanding of

Torah and our own special relationship to it. That, indeed, is what we celebrate on Shavuot.

"Why bother with any of this?" you may wonder in exasperation. "Wouldn't it be better to focus more on performing good deeds? All this emphasis on Torah study diverts attention from what we Jews really ought to be doing: working to achieve the social justice that the Torah mandates."

This is an important argument and an old one. It hearkens back to the days when the Romans occupied Palestine, and a debate on this very subject took place between two great Talmudic rabbis, one a proponent of study and the other a proponent of action.

Rabbi Tarfon argued, just as some do now, that action should take absolute precedence. Fulfilling God's commandments, such as caring for those in need and working to achieve social justice, should come first. Study, he believed, should come second.

Rabbi Akiba vehemently disagreed. Study should take precedence, he insisted. The reason, he explained, is that when study comes first, the fulfillment of God's commandments follows naturally.

The Talmud records that Rabbi Akiba's view won the day: "Study is greater, for it leads to action."

Study remains a high priority to this day for Jews, shared by those who disagree about almost everything else. In the United States, Jews spend over $1.5 billion annually on Jewish education—about $300 for every

Jewish man, woman, and child. Since learning is a life-long obligation, there are Jewish educational institutions and informal study communities for every age group.

The goal of all this education, however, is not just to become a learned Jew, but also, as Rabbi Akiba antici-pated, an active one. Judaism teaches that the more you know, the more you understand, and the more you un-derstand, the more you do. That is why Jews commemo-rate the giving of the Torah on Shavuot, and why, on this date, the committed and loving vows between the people of Israel and the Torah are symbolically renewed.

Love,
Abba

6

ANTISEMITISM

Tishah be-Av

Dear Leah,

Today is the ninth day of the Hebrew month of Av, known as Tishah be-Av, the saddest day in the entire Jewish calendar. While my neighbor heads for the beach (for it is 94 degrees here and humid), the people at my synagogue sit steeped in mourning, squatting on low stools or crouched on the floor. Many of the synagogue's ornaments have been temporarily removed, and the faithful remove their leather shoes and will neither eat nor drink for twenty-five hours. Instead of enjoying the beach, they will spend much of today reciting *kinot*, dirges and elegies. Last night, with lights dimmed, congregants chanted *Eicha*, the book of Lamentations from the Bible, to a haunting melody. "Alas," the book declares, "lonely sits the city, once great with people. . . . Bitterly she weeps in the night, her cheek wet with tears. There is none to comfort her."

Tishah be-Av originally commemorated tragic events that occurred more than twenty-five hundred years ago. The Babylonian army under King Nebuchadnezzar destroyed Jerusalem and its holy temple, built by King Solomon. They took many citizens of Judea captive, exiling them to Babylonia.

History, however, magnified the tragedies connected with this somber day so that over time it came to represent *all* Jewish catastrophes from biblical days to the present. On Tishah be-Av, according to tradition, God decreed that the Israelites who left Egypt following the Exodus would not enter the Promised Land; the Romans destroyed Judaism's Second Temple, built by King Herod; an anti-Roman revolt led by a brave general named Simeon Bar Kokhba was put down; crusaders massacred Jews; Parisians burned the Talmud; England (in 1290) and Spain (in 1492) expelled their Jews; World War I began, wreaking untold suffering upon Central and Eastern European Jews; and the first Jews were murdered at the Treblinka death camp.

Whether each of these events actually occurred precisely on the ninth of Av hardly matters. In Jewish memory, the fast of Tishah be-Av recalls all those who suffered or perished because they were Jews, as well as all Jews victimized by intolerance. Hatred of the Jew may well be humanity's greatest hatred, deeper, more universal, and longer-lasting than any other. On Tishah be-Av we mourn the victims of that hatred and seek consolation in God's promise of mercy and redemption.

"Why the Jews?" you ask. "Why have our people been so singled out for persecution?"

There are a great many answers to this question. According to the traditional liturgy, it is "on account of our sins." That is the clear message of the book of Lamentations, which declares that "Jerusalem has greatly sinned, therefore she is become a mockery." The lesson, for Jews, was to become self-critical. Before blaming others for our misfortunes, we are taught to look inward.

Of course, many a sinful people has not suffered nearly so much as Jews have. "Sometimes," as the Bible acknowledges, "a good man perishes in spite of his goodness, and sometimes a wicked one endures in spite of his wickedness." Besides, it is hard to imagine *any* sin that would justify thousands of years of persecution. However blameworthy Jews may have been for their misdeeds, an explanation that lays *all* the blame upon the victims rather than upon the persecutors leaves many questions unanswered.

Another explanation places the blame for antisemitism squarely on the fact that Judaism remains a living faith. According to this view, Judaism, by its very existence, poses a challenge to other faiths and nations—especially those like Christendom and Islam that believe *their* faith to be the only true one and themselves to be

Judaism's rightful heirs. A strong, vibrant Judaism threatens the most basic beliefs, values, and allegiances of Christians and Muslims. So long as Judaism exists, proponents of this view maintain, antisemitism is inevitable.

Still, a third explanation of antisemitism blames the phenomenon on "dislike of the unlike." Jews, throughout history, have been different from their neighbors: different in their beliefs and practices and often different in their language, occupations, and dress as well. As far back as the Bible, Jews were described as "a people that dwells apart," one "whose laws are different from those of any other people." In medieval times, they stood out in some countries by being "not Christian" and in other countries by being "not Muslim." Frequently, they chose for reasons of security and comfort to live in close proximity to other Jews, perhaps on a so-called Jew Street, such as the one that existed in Frankfurt, Germany, and the one that still exists in Kochi, India. Sometimes they actually were required to live apart, as in Rome or Prague, where one can still visit prescribed sections of town once known as the Jewish "ghetto."

Even now, wherever they live (except in Israel), Jews by virtue of being Jewish are unlike their neighbors. That is true, even here in America, where many a Christian is astonished to discover that Jews do not celebrate Christmas. Jews have suffered hatred and persecution through the centuries, according to this view, because we Jews are perennial nonconformists.

Scholars have advanced countless other theories of antisemitism: economic ones, religious ones, political ones, cultural ones, historical ones, sociological ones, psychological ones, and more. I'd be glad to recommend a few books to you, and we can discuss them. But although I suspect that all these theories are partly right, on Tishah be-Av none of them really matters. For the day properly focuses on the victims: the millions of innocent men, women, and children who have sacrificed their lives, through the years, simply on account of their faith. Emotionally, I find myself drawn less to the theorists and more to the eleventh-century poet Kalonymous ben Judah, whose elegy we recited this morning:

> *Oh . . . that I might weep continuously day and night over my slain children and infants, and the elders of my community. Wail along with me—alas and alack—shed copious tears. For the house of Israel, God's own people, felled by the sword.*

TISHAH BE-AV, HOWEVER, is about much more than just antisemitism. A good deal of the official liturgy of the day focuses on the destruction by the Romans of Judaism's Second Temple, dedicated in 515 BCE, enlarged and rebuilt by King Herod in the first century BCE, and destroyed by the Romans in the year 70. The temple, in its day, was the focal point of the Jewish religion and one of the world's most beautiful buildings. Its devastation meant the end of temple rituals and sacrifices, the loss of Jewish sovereignty (until the State of Israel was declared), and, for many, permanent exile.

We likewise recall on Tishah be-Av the self-destructive behavior that, according to tradition, brought about the Temple's destruction, particularly the baseless hatred of Jews for one another. There were Jews who sought accommodation with Rome and Jews who rebelled against the domination of Rome; Jews who considered themselves moderates and Jews who proclaimed themselves zealots. At one point, Jerusalem was divided into three warring sections, each one led by a proponent of some different Jewish ideology. Jews murdered other Jews; banditry and terrorism abounded; and the entire Jewish community was torn by factionalism and partisan rivalries. By the time the Roman general Titus arrived to put down the rebellion, the Jewish community was too divided to unite. The result was disaster.

Much can be learned from that disaster about the dangers of zealotry, factionalism, and baseless hatred. Still, two thousand years later, mourning the destruction of the Temple and the suspension of animal sacrifices is far from easy. You would not be alone if you wonder why we should still bother. Would anybody seek to restore Temple rituals and animal sacrifices?

Some Jews, it turns out, absolutely would. In fact, there are Jews in Jerusalem today who are preparing vigorously for the time when the "Third Temple" will be

rebuilt and sacrifices restored. Not only are they studying all the complex laws of the Temple service, they are
even fashioning the holy vessels and implements that
those rituals would require. The Bible and the Talmud
set forth the laws of sacrifices in elaborate detail. As Jews
who follow the Bible and the Talmud, they look forward
to the day when they will be able to carry out those laws,
in fulfillment of what they believe to be God's will. Next
time you visit Jerusalem, you can watch them busily at
work.

Other Jews, though, think that Judaism is much better off without a central Temple and animal sacrifices.
The destruction of Jerusalem made it possible for the
Jewish people to become "a kingdom of priests and a
holy nation," Reform Judaism classically believes. The
move from temple sacrifices to synagogue prayer and
from centralization to decentralization made it easier, according to this view, for the Jewish people to influence
humanity as a whole.

What I find remarkable, thinking about Tishah be-
Av, is that Judaism survived at all after its holiest shrine
was destroyed and its central rituals were suppressed.
Offhand, I cannot think of any other ancient religion that
did. The revolution that Judaism underwent following
the destruction of the Temple—its transformation into
Judaism as we know it—is nothing short of astonishing.
By limiting their mourning to Tisha be-Av and a few
shorter fast days, Jews managed to move past the tragedy

that had befallen them and to rebuild Judaism on a firm new basis, around the synagogue and rabbinic law.

Back in 1971, four years after the Western Wall (the remains of the ancient Temple in Jerusalem) came under Israeli sovereignty following the Six Day War, I met Jews who sought to abolish Tishah be-Av as a fast day. "Instead of mourning the destruction of Jerusalem, we should be celebrating the rebuilding of Jerusalem," one of them told me. It certainly seemed strange in those heady days to intone prayers that described Jerusalem as "the city that is in mourning and in ruins, despised and desolate," when in fact, Jerusalem was in the midst of a building boom and its Jewish population was burgeoning.

Yet through the years, as hopes for peace receded, factionalism among Jews grew, and suicide bombings and attacks on Jews in Jerusalem and around the world multiplied, Tishah be-Av has become more meaningful to me than ever. I look upon it as an annual reminder of destruction and renewal, of persecutions and martyrdom, of the dangers of baseless hatred and senseless death, and of commitment to life. It has become a day to reflect on the state of the Jewish people, past, present, and future.

Words found in a revised prayer for Tishah be-Av, composed in Israel after the Six Day War, match my sentiments exactly:

May all who mourn Jerusalem of old rejoice with her now. May they hear in the . . . streets of Jerusalem

sounds of joy and gladness, voices of bride and groom.
Grant peace to the city which You have redeemed, and
protect her.

"Enough about Israel! What about America?" you may
ask. "Surely its history with respect to Jews is altogether
different."

Indeed it is, and Tishah be-Av is a fine time to reflect
upon that too. Truth be told, though, there has been
plenty of prejudice against Jews in America, going all the
way back to 1654, when Peter Stuyvesant sought to bar
them from New Amsterdam. During the years when antisemitism crested in this country, during the half-
century prior to World War II, a Jew named Leo Frank
was lynched in Georgia for a crime he never committed;
Henry Ford spent part of his fortune spreading antise-
mitic propaganda and fulminating against "The International Jew: The World's Foremost Problem" (he later
apologized); and another national hero, Charles A. Lind-
bergh, accused Jews of disloyalty and blamed them for
leading America off to war. Millions of ordinary Jews in
those days (including some of your relatives) experienced
intense discrimination. They were limited in where they
could live, where they could study, where they could
work, where they could unwind, even where they could
go on vacation.

Nevertheless, in comparison to most other countries,
America *has* been unique in its history toward Jews. The

kinds of catastrophes recalled on Tishah be-Av have never happened here: no massacres, no large-scale expulsions, no forced conversions, and certainly no Holocaust. Others, notably people of African descent and Native Americans, were the ones who suffered most in America. Even if they suffered too, Jews, as a rule, benefited from the abundant opportunities that America opened up to them. For all the obstacles that they faced, many Jews prospered. The reality of anti-Jewish discrimination did not prevent them from gaining an education and clambering up the ladder to success.

How long this will continue, of course, nobody knows. During Tishah be-Av, we recall other times and places where Jews felt securely confident until history taught them otherwise. Spain, Germany, Poland, Russia—each welcomed Jews, won their hearts, and ultimately betrayed them. America, with its distinctive history, legal system, and mix of different ethnic and religious groups, may well prove different. But experience teaches us to be eternally vigilant. Complacency is a luxury that no Jew can afford.

That is why I find it appropriate to set one day aside each summer to contemplate the long chain of historical tragedies that has befallen the Jewish people. Draining as it is emotionally and physically, it also leaves me strangely uplifted. "How fortunate we are! How wonderful our destiny! How pleasant our lot!" a traditional

Jewish prayer declares. As Tishah be-Av comes to a close, I am reminded how very lucky we are to live where we do and when we do.

Here's hoping that you make the most of that good fortune!

Love,
Abba

7

LOVE, MARRIAGE, AND DECLINING NUMBERS

Tu be-Av

Dear Leah,

The question that you posed last night continues to echo in my head. "Why," you asked, "are Jews so morbid?" Just based on my recent letters, you noticed that "Passover recalls slavery, Yom ha-Shoah recalls the Holocaust, and Tishah be-Av recalls an endless history of bloody persecutions." Speaking, I suspect, for many of your generation, you wondered why Jews cannot simply "set the past aside and be happy?"

It did not occur to me last night when we spoke, but today, in antiquity, was actually one of the happiest days in the Jewish calendar. Nobody much remembers the holiday today, and I was not planning to inflict another long letter upon you so soon after Tishah be-Av. But given the coincidence of your question and today's holiday, I can scarcely restrain myself.

Tu be-Av (the fifteenth of Av), celebrated just six days after Tishah be-Av, marked the beginning of the vintage in ancient Israel, the season of gathering grapes for winemaking. "There were no holidays so joyous for the Jewish people," the Talmud relates. As part of the day's festivities, unmarried young women donned white garments borrowed from one another ("in order not to put to shame anyone who had none") and came to dance in the vineyards, brazenly calling out to eligible bachelors, "lift up your eyes and choose wisely."

To this day, Tu be-Av is considered a propitious day for a Jewish wedding. In some places in modern Israel, the day has turned into the Jewish equivalent of Valentine's Day and dubbed "the Festival of Love."

Why didn't they teach you these things in school? I suspect that your rabbis were a little embarrassed. In fact, the later commentators tried to explain the custom away, insisting (even though the text seems to say otherwise) that men and women danced separately and modestly.

Maybe the time has come, though, to revive this holiday. Judging from what I read about the burgeoning numbers of frustrated Jewish singles, a holiday devoted to the mysterious art of seduction might not be such a bad idea.

JEWISH TRADITION does not have anything good to say about singleness. The rabbis were impatient with single men ("He who has no wife lives without good, or help, or

joy, or blessing, or atonement. . . . He is also without life"),
and they pitied single women. Unlike their Christian
counterparts, they overwhelmingly opposed celibacy. How
can one be celibate and fulfill one of Judaism's cardinal
commandments, "Be fruitful and multiply?" Real happiness, tradition holds, reposes in family life, and it therefore
encourages marriage at an early age—the preferred age for
marriage, according to the rabbis, is eighteen. By contrast,
the deliberate renunciation of marriage, as among monks
and nuns, was little known and frowned upon. Religious
leaders in Judaism are *supposed* to be married.

"So most of us single folks are sinners. Thanks a lot!"
I hear you say.

But that is not quite what I mean. My point, simply, is
that in Jewish tradition, if you really want to be happy,
you get married. Three different blessings recited at a
Jewish wedding speak explicitly of joy, and—as anyone
who has ever been to a Jewish wedding knows—rejoicing
is what the wedding feast is all about. There are plenty of
other times during the year when Jews are enjoined to be
happy, including the Hebrew month of Adar, when the
holiday of Purim falls. But only in connection with a
wedding do we speak of "joy and gladness . . . mirth and
exultation, pleasure and delight, love, brotherhood, peace
and fellowship." In Judaism, life doesn't get any better
than that!

Once upon a time, almost every Jew got married.
That was the only legitimate way to have sex, the only

way to find companionship, the only way to have children, and the only way (in the eyes of the Jewish community) to be fulfilled as a person. In some cases, young people chose their own life partners; in other cases, their parents chose for them; and in still other cases matchmakers, for a fee, put the man and the woman together. The rate of success, alas, was probably no better than it is today. Making a good match, the rabbis declare, is as difficult as parting the Red Sea.

The problem, in the world that we live in, is that marriage is fast going out of style. Fewer than 60 percent of Americans over the age of eighteen are currently married, down from 80 percent a generation ago. Among Jews, the number may still be lower. One study found that 59 percent of U.S. Jews who identify religiously are married, and only 45 percent of those who do not identify religiously have married. In Boston, where I live, more than a third of all Jewish households now consist of unmarried adults. Those who do get married, moreover, tend to do so later—not at eighteen, as the rabbis advised, but closer to thirty-six. And even then, many of them go on to get divorced.

I worry about this for two reasons. First, Judaism is very family- and home-oriented. Holiness and home life overlap. The Sabbath, household rituals, holidays—all are very difficult to observe on one's own but are beautiful and meaningful in the presence of family. I know that plenty of singles get together for religious celebrations, but in my experience such gatherings, pleasant as they are, do not substitute for family gatherings. Nor do they promote the kind of intergenerational ties upon which Jewish continuity depends.

Second, I worry that we Jews are failing to reproduce ourselves. A nationwide survey that I read reports that at every age group, Jewish women have fewer children than their non-Jewish counterparts. More than half of all Jewish women have not had their first child by the age of thirty-four (by which time your great-grandmother was already the mother of seven children). The average total number of children born to Jewish women today is less than 1.9—substantially below the 2.1 deemed necessary just for a population to remain stable. The conclusion of the study could scarcely be more dire: Jews are not reproducing themselves fast enough to replace today's Jewish population.

I can already hear you and your friends howling in protest. "Jewish women are not baby machines!" "Well-educated professional women want careers, not just pregnancies!" "Who can afford children?" "The number of Jews may be declining, but the planet as a whole is over-populated!" "Focus on the quality of Jewish life; the numbers will take care of themselves!"

Believe me, I appreciate all these arguments. Nobody believes more strongly than I do in educating Jewish women, as well as men, for fulfilling professional lives. That is why I spent so much money on your own schooling. Nor am I under any illusions about how difficult and expensive it is to raise children properly (been there, done that!). I even worry, as you do, about global overpopulation.

I hope, though, that you do not underestimate the significance of family—the one that you are part of and the one that I hope you will someday raise. Families link us backward and forward in time; they support us in good times and bad; they constitute our greatest legacy to the future; and, at least in our case, they have been a wondrous source of pride and joy. No accomplishment of ours in the professional world comes close to the satisfaction we have had in watching you and your brother grow up. Admittedly, meeting family responsibilities and balancing them with professional ones has not always been easy. But nothing truly worthwhile ever is.

Even though we produced two children, a lot fewer than some of our fervently Orthodox relatives did, I do *not* agree that, in Jewish life, numbers are irrelevant, much less that our declining numbers "will take care of themselves." More than sixty years after the Holocaust, the worldwide Jewish population still has not recovered. Where once there were eighteen million Jews worldwide, now there are only about thirteen million. Outside of Israel, only 1.2 of every thousand people in the world is Jewish, probably the smallest percentage of the world that we have been in more than two thousand years. We are—let's face it—a tiny drop in the world's bucket. Our numbers are less than the statistical error in the Chinese census. And every single year, as fewer Jews marry and fewer married Jews have children, the Jewish population outside Israel shrinks a little bit further.

Jews today are nothing less than an endangered people. You have friends who work to rescue endangered animal and plant species, so you know why this matters. Recognizing the value of diversity, we labor to preserve threatened and endangered species lest they vanish from the face of the earth, thereby diminishing us all. In the case of the bald eagle, our efforts to "protect, enhance, and increase" its numbers succeeded quite handsomely. Now, we need to similarly "protect, enhance, and increase" the Jewish people.

Remember the Huguenots, members of the French Reformed church, who once were much more numerous than Jews in the United States? We visited a beautiful old Huguenot church a few years ago; it commemorates their heritage. Well, the Huguenots failed to maintain their distinctive faith and culture, intermarried in large numbers, and disappeared as an independent religious community. What was once a vibrant Huguenot culture is now largely a memory. We surely would not want that to happen to us!

Tu be-Av, once one of our most joyous holidays and now mostly forgotten, may be an appropriate day to consider what to do. We can ignore the numbers and risk disappearing, or we can work to increase our numbers by marrying and having more children.

Lift up your eyes and choose wisely!

Love,
Abba

8

JUDGMENT WITHOUT RESOLUTION

Rosh Hashanah

Dear Leah,

It's the birthday of the world! On Rosh Hashanah, the first day of the Hebrew month of Tishri, the Jewish year begins, and, according to Jewish tradition, the world was born. Rosh Hashanah marks the anniversary of creation itself.

Years ago, when I served as a high holiday cantor, I would begin preparing weeks in advance for Rosh Hashanah. Early in the morning and at night when I returned from work, I would practice the traditional high holiday music. Reviewing the melodies, some of them dating back centuries or more (tradition dates some of them all the way back to the giving of the Torah on Mount Sinai!) always felt like a reunion with old friends. Even now, they help put me in the proper mood for the holiday; I have been humming them for days.

My brother, growing up, blew the shofar, the traditional ram's horn sounded during the service. Its piercing blasts echoed through our house during his practice sessions. Not only could we hear them, but we could actually feel them vibrating through us. The shofar is not my favorite musical instrument, but it serves its purpose. It announces that the new year approaches and calls upon us to reflect and repent.

The book of Numbers actually calls Rosh Hashanah the "day of trumpeting." It knows nothing of Rosh Hashanah as such and assigns our holiday to the first day of the *seventh* month; the biblical new year fell in spring. But under the influence of cultures that celebrated the new year in the autumn, in conjunction with the late harvest, a debate apparently took place. One great rabbi taught that the world was created in the month of Tishri in the fall, and another taught that it was created in the month of Nisan in the spring. In the end, Jewish tradition sided with the fall date. So what the Bible called the "day of trumpeting" became, by the time of the Second Temple, Rosh Hashanah—new year—the birthday of the world and the day when all humanity is judged.

A whole tractate of the Talmud focuses on the laws and practices of the day, particularly the laws concerning the blowing of the shofar and the day's distinctive prayers. The Talmud also explains how spotters watched for the new moon, which marks the beginning of the holiday and of the new year. Owing to questions concerning when the new moon actually appeared, which is difficult to determine with the naked eye, what was originally a one-day holiday soon morphed into two—just to be sure. Today, of course, such doubts have long since been resolved, and in place of moon watchers, Judaism relies upon a fixed calendar. Many Reform Jews, as a result, celebrate the festival for only one day.

The rabbis could not agree over the precise chronology of the distant past. The age of the world posed something of a mystery to them. Finally, some nine hundred years ago, learned rabbis concluded, based on biblical and other sources, that forty-eight hundred years had passed since creation. By their calculation God said "Let there be light" on the Rosh Hashanah equivalent of what would have been October 7, 3761 BCE. Jewish years, even now, are counted from that momentous day—supposedly the first day of the first year in the history of the world. We are now, by this count, in the world's sixth post-creation millennium.

Modern science, of course, dates creation ("the big bang") a lot less precisely—and some ten to twenty billion years earlier. Some people lose a great deal of sleep over this and strive mightily to reconcile scientific findings and Jewish tradition.

Not me!

Science, to my mind, primarily seeks to understand when and how the world came about. Judaism asks us to take stock of the world and of our own place within it.

Science explores the age of the world, Judaism, the state of the world. The two sometimes complement one another, but their questions, methods, and assumptions could not be more different. In the final analysis, Judaism does not experiment, and science does not judge.

The fact that Judaism and modern science disagree over the age of the world, therefore, bothers me not in the slightest. Scientifically speaking, science is right. Jewishly speaking, Judaism is right.

Because Rosh Hashanah *is* for Jews a day of judging, Jews do not celebrate the "birthday of the world" with a rollicking party. There are no balloons, no fireworks, no late-night revelries. Instead, the mood of the day is summed up in a pithy Hebrew prayer: "Today is the birthday of the world. Today all the world's creatures stand in judgment."

Judgment, indeed, is the central metaphor of Rosh Hashanah. On that day, according to tradition, our fate is inscribed. Ten days later, on Yom Kippur, it is sealed:

How many shall pass away and how many shall be
   born,
Who shall live and who shall die
Who shall reach the end of his days and who shall not

Seeking to be judged worthy of a good new year, a prosperous year, a year of health and well-being, Jews like me spend hours in a synagogue on Rosh Hashanah—the morning service alone usually takes five hours to complete. We atone humbly for our sins and pray devoutly for our lives. In advance of Rosh Hashanah, many of us also contribute generously to charity. Having been taught that "penitence, prayer, and righteous deeds avert the evil decree," we do all that we can to produce a positive outcome, much like a defendant preparing to be sentenced.

"Surely you don't believe any of that rot," an uninhibited student interjected when he overheard me talking about this subject.

"If everyone believed it," I shot back, "our world would be much better off."

The student was astounded, so I took the opportunity to explain. Rosh Hashanah, I said, uses the theme of divine judgment to reinforce three central ideas that are as necessary today as ever they have been: (1) human frailty, (2) freedom, and (3) responsibility for your own life choices.

First, I told him, Rosh Hashanah makes the point that human beings—kings, queens, presidents, prime ministers, business tycoons, rabbis, principals, and the rest of us, to the lowliest pauper—are mere flesh-and-blood mortals. That's why Jews so often find the courage to speak truth to power. High positions and fancy titles do not impress us. Tradition emphasizes the majesty of God, before whom "all things lie exposed," as an antidote to human arrogance and conceit.

In addition, Rosh Hashanah underscores the autonomy of human beings, their freedom to choose between right and wrong, good and evil, suitable behavior and sinful behavior. The holiday presupposes that people who have done wrong can confess, repent, and change their ways, transforming themselves and, potentially, the world. Human destiny is not predestined, and it's never too late to change course. However much God may foresee, "freedom of choice is granted."

Finally, Rosh Hashanah holds people responsible for their own actions. Nobody escapes judgment, the liturgy of the holiday insists. Only those who own up to their personal misdeeds, apologize for them, and pledge to change can hope to find mercy. For that reason, during the days leading up to Rosh Hashanah and on through Yom Kippur, Jews repeatedly confess their sins and beg forgiveness ("We have sinned against Thee, our God; forgive us, our Creator"). Naming our misdeeds and sins and accepting responsibility for them is a necessary first step on the road to reform.

My student, to say the least, was nonplussed. He admitted that he always thought that Rosh Hashanah was simply about the desire to live on for another year. He recalled the story that three books are opened in heaven on new year, one for the thoroughly wicked, one for the thoroughly righteous, and one for those in between whose fate is decided on Yom Kippur. It never occurred to him that there was more to the holiday than that.

I am hoping that our conversation will stimulate him to learn more about Judaism. In a sense, that too is what Rosh Hashanah is about: improvement, progress, the resolve to do better.

Last year at this time, one person I know pledged to study a traditional Jewish text every day. Another resolved to begin every workday by reciting morning prayers. A third promised to light Sabbath candles every Friday night. A fourth vowed to keep kosher. Not all of these resolutions lasted (neither do secular new year's resolutions), but Rosh Hashanah serves, nevertheless, as an annual holiday of revival among Jews. It brings back into the synagogue some who have not visited in a year and stimulates others to deepen their Jewish knowledge and connection and strengthen their Jewish practices.

Friends of mine remain skeptical. The Jewish world, they believe, is on an inevitable downward slope. As they watch their children intermarry and abandon religious practices, they complain that every generation is less Jewish than its predecessor.

I, by contrast, have faith. I know that some Jews are more observant of tradition than their parents, others less. Some are religious seekers, perennially in quest of spiritual highs. Many evolve religiously throughout their lifetimes, moving now in one direction, now in another as their Jewish journeys proceed. For all these Jews, Rosh Hashanah serves as a way station, an annual stop for self-evaluation and community connection, a reminder that revitalization and renewal remain ever possible.

Time and again, rebellious Jews whom some would have written off entirely have turned out to be agents of communal transformation. Think of Franz Rosenzweig, the great German-Jewish philosopher, who contemplated conversion to Christianity in 1913, found inspiration and God in a high holiday service in Berlin, and went on to become the preeminent inspiration for Germany's prewar Jewish renaissance. Think of Louis Brandeis, the great American lawyer and Supreme Court justice, who barely associated with his fellow Jews for the first fifty-four years of his life, yet emerged on the eve of World War I as the leader of American Zionism. Even in my lifetime, some Jewish radicals who battled the establishment in their twenties, and were described as exhibiting irredeemable self-hatred, went on to became transformative leaders of the Jewish community. Based on this past experience, I never write Jews off.

"But what about writing God off?" some may defiantly ask. "Rosh Hashanah works fine for those who believe in God's majesty, but what about those who do not? Their numbers, after all, are growing."

Actually, plenty of secular Jews do observe Rosh Hashanah. A major theme of the holiday concerns self-improvement. No need to believe in God to believe in that! The Congress of Secular Jewish Organizations, perhaps anticipating this question, insists that secular Jews can observe Rosh Hashanah perfectly well without God:

> *The ethical component of Rosh Hashanah is the most important aspect of the holiday for secular Jews. It is a time for self-reflection and evaluation; a time to admit our failings and take stock of our conduct. It is a time to commit ourselves to the repair of the world or tikkun olam, beginning in our personal relationships and extending outward to the Jewish and non-Jewish communities. The sound of the shofar, so intimately associated with Rosh Hashanah, can be heard as a clarion call to assume these responsibilities.*

The more difficult question concerns those who do believe in God but question His justice. Why, they wonder, echoing Rabbi Harold Kushner, do bad things happen to good people? Like Abraham in the Bible, they ask, "Shall not the Judge of all the earth deal justly?"

Holocaust survivor Elie Wiesel described his own struggle with this question on the Rosh Hashanah that he spent in the concentration camp of Auschwitz, where he was incarcerated:

> *Once, New Year's Day had dominated my life. I knew that my sins grieved the Eternal; I implored his forgiveness. Once, I had believed profoundly that upon*

one solitary deed of mine, one solitary prayer, depended the salvation of the world.

This day, I had ceased to plead. I was no longer capable of lamentation. On the contrary, I felt very strong. I was the accuser, God the accused. My eyes were open and I was alone—terribly alone in a world without God and without man.

For me, the same difficult question arose when I was diagnosed with esophageal cancer. The Rosh Hashanah that followed was the most difficult of my life. You were very young then, which only made the whole situation harder. Never had the question "who shall live and who shall die" seemed so personally and painfully relevant.

One rabbi advised that even in the face of adversity, my job was to sanctify God's name. Just as so many generations of Jews had countered powerful and oppressive religious adversaries with spiritual resistance, said he, I now needed to fight powerful and oppressive physical adversaries, like cancer, in the same way. "Resist!" he cried, "don't give up!" Fighting and praying for life on Rosh Hashanah, he declared, is the best means of staving off death and living up to what Judaism teaches.

A learned friend offered different advice: just accept the hand that God has dealt you. You are grateful for the good things that happen; accept the bad in the same spirit. No fighting, no groveling, no bargaining. Once the sentence comes down, he opined, our job as mere mortals is simply to affirm, "Blessed be the true Judge."

Still a third friend, quoting his philosopher-father, compared my predicament to a spiritual test. In the Bible, God tested Abraham ten different times, according to tradition. Each time, the challenge spurred Abraham to action. He became, in a sense, God's partner. Fighting cancer, my friend declared, likewise required an act of partnering. If I responded to the challenge vigorously and with all the means at my disposal, God would do the rest.

Taking all these responses together and reconciling them seemed to me, at first glance, an impossible task. Why couldn't Judaism give me a straightforward answer when I most needed one? That year, as you fortunately do not remember, I approached Rosh Hashanah in a contentious mood.

Thinking about it later, however, I realized that the multiplicity of answers was in fact the right answer. Jewish tradition is too long, too deep, and too sophisticated to be satisfied with simple responses to timeless and difficult theological conundrums. In my case, as in so many others, there can be no single answer. That may be why the penitential prayers culminate with the idea that human beings are limited. God alone knows "the mysteries of the universe and the things hidden from mortal eyes," and God is not about to tell.

Love,
Abba

9

THE INDIVIDUAL AND
THE COMMUNITY

Yom Kippur

Dear Leah,

Always a great joy to hear from you. I am thrilled to learn that you made it to synagogue on Rosh Hashanah, and sorry to hear that the rabbi's sermon proved so uninspiring. Poor rabbis! Some of them work all summer composing their high holiday sermons, the most important sermons that they deliver all year. The pressure to say not only the right thing but *everything* that congregants need to hear can be overwhelming. Personally, I prefer the less formal talks our rabbi delivers later in the year, when all the pressure subsides.

This evening there will be another huge crowd at the synagogue. The fast day of Yom Kippur, the Day of Atonement, starts at dusk with the service known as Kol Nidrei, named for a prayer that retracts hastily made vows. You probably remember the haunting tune to which the Kol Nidrei prayer is sung. It is among the most moving (as well as the most ancient) pieces of music in our entire liturgy. I try never to miss it, for it sets a tone for the whole of Yom Kippur.

Your mother and I will rush over to Kol Nidrei straight from a big meal. The key, I have learned, is to drink a great deal of water at this "last meal," for we can neither eat nor drink again until the fast ends tomorrow at nightfall. Some will spend the bulk of the intervening hours in the synagogue itself. There they renew ties with the Jewish community, seek atonement for sins, and vow to improve.

Taking time off in the middle of the week to observe Yom Kippur is, I know, not easy—especially for those with demanding schedules. Back when I was growing up, we all were impressed by pitcher Sandy Koufax of the Los Angeles Dodgers, who sat out the opening game of the World Series game in 1965, rather than pitch on Yom Kippur. Some folks, though, never forgave him—especially when the Dodgers lost the game! They believed that his first loyalty should have been to his team.

The same debate took place in 2004, you'll remember, involving slugger Shawn Green. With his Los Angeles Dodgers team in a tight pennant race, *two* critical games coincided with Yom Kippur. Green played in the evening game and sat out the afternoon game. What would you have done in his place?

Balancing work with the rest of life is never easy—not for those who observe Yom Kippur, or other Jewish holidays, or the Sabbath, or the laws of keeping kosher, or indeed, for those with *any* serious commitment outside work. Even balancing family and work, I can tell you, is often a supreme challenge. Nevertheless, conflicts, painful as they may be, help us to clarify our priorities in life. Yom Kippur is as good a day as any to figure out what those priorities should be. In the end, only you can decide whether Yom Kippur is one of them.

What I can tell you is that Yom Kippur has been, for thousands of years, the holiest, most solemn day in the entire Jewish calendar. "On this day shall atonement be made for you to cleanse you," the Bible declares. Once a year, on Yom Kippur, the high priest dramatically entered the "holy of holies" in the ancient temple. There he invoked God's secret name and confessed the sins of himself, his family, his fellow priests, and all the community of Israel. Hearing God's name, the people fell on their faces, crying, "Blessed be God's glorious kingdom forever and ever."

The high priest is no more, and God's secret name has been lost, but Yom Kippur remains all about atonement. The high priest's ritual, evocatively described in some of the prayers, may today be only a distant memory, but the drumbeat of wrongs in need of righting could have been written yesterday. Two different confessional prayers are repeated over and over on Yom Kippur. Both are alphabetical, conveying the sense that we need to atone, literally, for every misdeed from A to Z.

Here are some excerpts, loosely translated from the original Hebrew:

> *We abuse, we betray, we are cruel.*
> *We destroy, we embitter, we falsify.*
> *We gossip, we hate, we insult.*
> *We jeer, we kill, we lie.*
> *We mock, we neglect, we oppress.*
> *We pervert, we quarrel, we rebel.*
> *We steal, we transgress, we are unkind.*
> *We are violent, we are wicked, we are xenophobic.*
> *We yield to evil, we are zealots for bad causes.*
>
> *For all of these, O God of forgiveness, forgive us, pardon us, grant us atonement.*

What never ceases to impress me about these prayers is their focus on "we" and "us," rather than "I" and "me." What Yom Kippur defines as sins—even crimes like robbery, violence, and licentiousness—are seen as the responsibility of the entire community. For this reason, rather than just confessing individually and in solitude, we confess together and in public. However much individuals are responsible for their own transgressions, the rest of us, the prayer suggests, are not wholly blameless.

This idea nicely meshes with Judaism's whole communitarian ethos. Being Jewish, for most of Jewish history, meant living in a community and making oneself subservient to communal discipline. "Separate not yourself from the community," the rabbis taught. From birth and naming rites to funeral rites, the defining moments that mark a Jew's life are experienced in a communal setting. Prayer too takes on special sanctity when performed in a group. Communal prayer with a *minyan* (prayer quorum) has a higher religious status in Judaism than the solitary prayer of an individual. Celebrating Yom Kippur on one's own is almost unthinkable.

Some Jews today have a great deal of trouble with Judaism's focus on the community. They celebrate individualism, the great American Lone Ranger ideal. The claim that they should hold themselves responsible for the sins of other Jews; that they should conform to the norms of the Jewish community; that they should consider Jews everywhere part of their extended family, take pride in their achievements, feel abashed at their misdeeds, and assist them in times of need—all this repels them. They prefer being Jewish at home to going to a synagogue. And they hate the idea that all Jews everywhere are their relatives. "We are no longer a tribe," they complain. They consider Jewish peoplehood a concept that has outlived its time.

"I don't regard the Jewish people as my family," one young Jewish activist has provocatively written. About half of American Jews, according to a poll, agree. Even fewer feel that "I have a special responsibility to take care of Jews in need around the world." A great many Jews still pray with other Jews on Yom Kippur, but

Jewish peoplehood, mutual responsibility, and the related ideas that Jews subsume under the rubric of *klal yisrael* (the community of Israel) are, it seems, endangered Jewish values.

This greatly saddens me. I love the idea that Judaism privileges the group over the individual. It helps to combat selfishness and self-centeredness. Moreover, the traditional precept that "all Jews are responsible for one another," whether they know them or not, like them or not, agree with them or not, simply because all Jews are family is, to me, an amazing concept. It is without parallel in Christianity or Islam.

Millions of Jews around the world are alive today because other Jews—who never had set eyes upon them but felt a sense of kinship toward them as fellow Jews—reached out to save them, or their ancestors, during times of persecution. Even in my lifetime, the successful movements to save Soviet Jews and Ethiopian Jews relied on this deeply felt feeling of mutual responsibility. It has saved more lives than any other Jewish value I can think of.

Do you remember when we were on vacation in Denmark and met an Israeli at the hotel who was all alone with nowhere to eat on Saturday? We had never set eyes on him before, but remembering that "all Jews are responsible for one another," we invited him to join us for lunch. I still recall how happy he was to share lunch in our room—and then it turned out that we even had friends in common! All of us had a much more enjoyable and memorable Sabbath meal thanks to that act of Jewish connection. It illustrates what Jewish peoplehood is all about.

A man I know was convicted of a white-collar financial crime and served a short term in a prison camp of about 120 people, about 25 percent of whom were Jews. "The non-Jews were all jealous," he reported. "We were a community that supported one another, ate together, took care of each other—regardless of level of observance, party affiliation or other potentially divisive factors."

"I needed to go to jail," he confessed, "to properly understand the concept that 'all Jews are responsible for one another.'"

So far from being outmoded, a sense of shared peoplehood seems to me to be something that others might want to learn from our example. What do you think? Wouldn't our world be much better off if everyone felt and acted the same way toward all members of *their* respective faiths?

"But why not treat *all* human beings as family?" you may protest. "Why privilege people who have nothing more in common with us than religion and ethnicity?"

As an ideal, I too consider universalism to be wonderfully noble. That is what Jews pray for at every service: the day "when the world will be perfected under the dominion of the Almighty." Practically speaking, though, just expanding people's sense of family to embrace members of their entire faith community would be a great achievement. Surely we need to consider our own people as family before we can reasonably advance to embrace other peoples around the world!

So I consider the communitarian emphasis of Yom Kippur to be a wonderful feature of Judaism, especially in a country like ours where rugged individualism is so commonly celebrated. By reinforcing communal ideals and focusing upon Jews as a group, Yom Kippur reinforces the basis of Jewish life as a whole.

I can hear you giggling. Wasn't I the person who recommended that you read a book called *Jew vs. Jew*? Surely I, of all people, know that Jews are deeply divided and have been for millennia. Today the disputes tend to pit different Jewish religious movements against one another or religious Jews against secular Jews. Over the past few centuries, Jewish communities have divided over false messiahs, over the pietistic movement known as Hasidism, over approaches to the enlightenment, over communism, over Zionism. The ideal of communal unity clashes with self-evident reality.

You may also not be fully persuaded by the claim that, no matter how divided, all Jews are family. Even I know that this raises as many questions as it answers. Does the Jewish community include members of *all* Jewish movements? Gay, lesbian, and transgendered Jews? Intermarried Jews? Children of Jewish fathers but not Jewish mothers? Non-Orthodox converts to Judaism?

When it comes right down to it, how inclusive *is* the Jewish community?

Like most difficult questions, these admit of no easy answer. Barrels of ink have been spilled on the subject of "who is a Jew," but for all that Jewish law has to say about the subject, no consensus has been reached. Perhaps this is not surprising. Large groups almost inevitably include some percentage of people whose status is uncertain. There are those who consider themselves members but are not so regarded by others. There are those whom others consider to be members but do not so regard themselves. Even our country has many "undocumented citizens," who view their relationship to the government differently than the government views its relationship to them. For most Jews, nevertheless, "self-identity" and "ascribed identity" amount to the same thing. But I agree with you that there are far too many people for whom, unfortunately, that is not the case.

Nevertheless, the theory of Yom Kippur is that on this day we put aside our differences and disputes and embrace the *entire* community. Even a heinous sinner (however that may be defined) is explicitly included in the day's prayers. In fact, the very first sentence in the traditional Yom Kippur liturgy declares that "we sanction prayer with the transgressors"—their presence among us does not invalidate our prayers. The great Orthodox Jewish philosopher, Rabbi Joseph B. Soloveitchik, went even further. "The communal atonement effected by the very day of Yom Kippur," he declared, "is compromised if *any* members of the Jewish people are excluded." Admittedly, his statement does not answer the question of *who* is a member of the Jewish people, but given this admonition, one would surely want to err on the side of caution and be as inclusive as possible!

So no matter how divided Jews are the rest of the year, and notwithstanding the many disagreements concerning "who is a Jew," Yom Kippur encourages us to focus on the ideal of an all-embracing Jewish community, one from which no member is excluded. Difficult problems remain, but maybe if we push hard enough on that ideal during Yom Kippur, we can make progress turning it into reality during the year ahead.

A PSYCHOLOGIST FRIEND OF MINE views Yom Kippur in less ideal terms. Indeed, he is deeply critical of some of the holiday's central assumptions. He thinks that religion should liberate human beings, rather than making them feel guilty. He also insists that individuals should assume responsibility for their own actions, rather than blaming them on the community. Where Yom Kippur starkly differentiates right from wrong, he believes that most human actions are much more complicated. "Where is it written," he asks, "that my morality is the same as yours?"

These arguments, I admit, contain much merit, but to my mind Yom Kippur is less the problem than the solution. The whole point of Yom Kippur, after all, is atonement, not guilt. The day is described by one traditional source as one of "forgiveness and expiation for Israel." We may enter the day feeling guilty, but Yom Kippur itself is supposed to leave us feeling purged and cleansed, "a newly made creature," as one ancient rabbi put it. In that sense, the day is just what my psychologist friend thinks it should be: liberating. At least for those who take it seriously.

As for individual responsibility, the tradition is more in agreement with contemporary psychology than my friend realizes. "For transgressions that are between a man and his fellow," the Talmud teaches, "the Day of Atonement effects atonement only if he has appeased his fellow." We may confess our sins as a group, but that does not free us from the need to beg the pardon of those we have wronged and to make restitution if required. Even private sins between a human being and God, according to tradition, require personal repentance for atonement to be effective.

Where my friend and I strongly disagree is in his defense of moral relativism. Philosophers may argue as to whether people everywhere share a common morality and whether it is legitimate to judge other peoples by our moral standards. Some dispute the very idea of "universal human rights." But do we really want to live in a community where moral judgments are forbidden since my morality may not be the same as yours? Must we give up on the whole idea of moral improvement? Can't some of us, at least, agree among ourselves to uphold a set of standards that we think right?

When I stand with my fellow congregants tonight and tomorrow, I uphold the proposition that we Jews, at least, *do* share common standards of morality. That is why we pray together and atone together for evils ranging, as we have seen, from abuse to zealotry. We read together two long lists of evils that we condemn as sins, and collectively seek forgiveness for the damage they have wrought on our community.

I understand perfectly well that agreement on ethical and moral questions is not easy to achieve. Consensus concerning a whole range of issues, from what constitutes life to how to define the moment of death, still eludes us. "Truth," the president of Harvard University recently observed, "is an aspiration, not a possession."

Nevertheless, on Yom Kippur I affirm my fervent hope that Jews—and someday all human beings—*will* reach consensus. We will learn to distinguish right from wrong. We will find truth and discard falsehood. We will ultimately become one in the values that we espouse and in the moral teachings that we uphold.

Do I sound too confident? Strangely, Yom Kippur inspires such confidence. That is why we dress in white rather than black on the holiday and why much of the music of the day is uplifting. In antiquity, Yom Kippur was actually a *joyous* holiday, compared by one ancient source to the holiday of Tu be-Av, the subject of an earlier letter. The reason is that those who atone for their sins feel purged and purified. An ancient rabbinic homily actually quotes God as promising that "whenever Israel gather in My presence and stand before Me as one band, crying out in My presence the order of prayers for forgiveness, I shall answer them." God, in Jewish tradition, is much more magnanimous than punitive. If only more people were like that too!

Over and over, therefore, Jews recite the attributes of God set forth in the book of Exodus, stressing that God forgives "iniquity, transgression, and sin." Some repeat this as many as twelve or twenty times during the day; one rabbi insisted that it should be repeated sixty-five times! The idea is not only to ensure God's affirmative response to our petition for forgiveness, but also to encourage emulation of God's moral qualities: compassion, graciousness, forbearance, kindness, faithfulness, and forgiveness. By becoming more Godlike, Judaism believes, we will all become better human beings.

So confident are we Jews in God's moral qualities, mercy in particular, that by the conclusion of Yom Kippur we are ready to breathe a sigh of relief. When you were young, you waited for that theatrical moment. You watched the sun setting and counted down until, at last, the shofar sounded. "Next year in Jerusalem," you cried out, along with the congregation. Then you joined those who, despite a day of fasting, gathered their strength to break out spontaneously in song and dance.

Confidence, of course, is more than just the secret of Yom Kippur. It is the secret of the Jewish people as a whole. Absent confidence, we Jews would long ago have succumbed to the many persecutors who sought to destroy us. Confidence, even in the darkest days of the Holocaust, kept Jews going.

Of course, there is also such a thing as overconfidence. That is why I worry so much about your generation. Some of your friends, I fear, worry much less than they should about the survival of Judaism, the survival of the State of Israel, and the continuity of the Jewish people as a whole. Complacency, I have told you before, is a luxury that no Jew can afford.

Nevertheless, the message of Yom Kippur and the lessons of Jewish history give me great cause for confidence. So long as Jews sound the shofar, so long as they cry, "Next year in Jerusalem," so long as they learn from the past and work to shape the future, so long as they juggle Judaism among their priorities, so long as they maintain a strong sense of family and community, and so long as they aspire to uphold common values and teachings, I am confident that the people of Israel will live on.

Love,
Abba

MAKING CHOICES AND IMPROVING THE WORLD

Sukkot

Dear Leah,

We are moving into a hut! Your mother and I put up the canvas structure this morning, and we have just added the pine needles and bamboo for the roof. I still have to put up electric lights and decorations. If all goes well and there is no rain, we will eat our first meal there tomorrow night.

We are not, of course, selling the house. Nor are we moving very far or for very long. Instead, as in years past, the hut on the back patio will be our official home for seven days, during the holiday of Sukkot.

The word "sukkot" (singular, sukkah) has been translated as huts, booths, and tabernacles. "You shall live in Sukkot seven days; all citizens in Israel shall live in Sukkot," the Bible declares. These huts, in ancient times, may have been functional. Farm workers lived in such temporary abodes during the fall harvest, so that they could spend every moment from morning till night in the fields gathering the crops.

In the Bible, though, the holiday of Sukkot took on added historical significance. The huts called to mind the experience of the children of Israel when they wandered for forty years in the desert. God personally set forth the pedagogic goal "that future generations may know that I made the Israelite people live in Sukkot when I brought them out of the land of Egypt."

Nowadays, Sukkot represents something of an "alternative lifestyle" for suburban folks like us. Communing so intimately with nature, eating for seven days in a fragile, temporary abode open to the elements, looking up at night to see stars twinkling through the thatched roof—these provide a mighty contrast to the sturdy, well-insulated homes we enjoy all the rest of the year. Dwelling in the Sukkah for a week, I find, changes my perception of what home means for our family and for those less fortunate than our family.

SUKKOT FALLS JUST FIVE DAYS after Yom Kippur. Inevitably, this gives rise to a question: How can one be Jewish and get any work done in the month of Tishri? Traditional Jews celebrate seven out of the month's first twenty-three days as holidays—plus intervening Sabbath days, when rest is likewise mandated. Keeping up with a job during the fall holiday season—and making up work for the Jewish holidays one takes off—is no small challenge. Of course, nobody ever said that living as a Jew amid a community of non-Jews would be easy!

It is so much simpler for our relatives in Israel. There, work practically screeches to a halt during the weeks from Rosh Hashanah to the end of Sukkot. Religious and secular Jews alike—albeit in different ways—celebrate the holiday season and consider it vacation time (much like the last weeks of December here in the United States). The rhythm of the Israeli year harmonizes easily with the Jewish calendar, whereas the American calendar's rhythm is decidedly Christian.

I suspect, though, that for many Jews the decision about observing Sukkot is not just based on proximity to the high holidays. The whole concept of a "harvest festival" fails to elicit much excitement. The great joy that once accompanied bountiful harvests, back in the days when bountiful harvests meant full bellies all winter long, now elicits only wonder. In today's global economy, harvests matter much less than they once did. Harvests in the land of Israel (which is about one-seventh the size of the state of Nebraska) hardly affect the worldwide food supply at all.

Besides, many of us celebrate another harvest festival every year, Thanksgiving Day, which we share with all Americans. Although the claim that the Puritans modeled Thanksgiving Day on Sukkot is a myth, Thanksgiving does remind us, as our Jewish holiday also does, to be grateful for the blessings of abundance. Why, then, do your mother and I continue to celebrate Sukkot, miss work, and spend seven days in a hut?

For a time, my best answer was, "That is what our tradition teaches us to do," an answer that I know you will not find fully satisfying. But reading the teachings of Philo of Alexandria, a Jewish philosopher of the first century, suggested to me new meanings for Sukkot.

For one thing, Philo explained, living in a hut teaches humility:

> It is well in wealth to remember your poverty; in distinction, your insignificance; in high offices, your position as a commoner; in peace, your dangers in war; on land, the storms on sea; in cities, the life of loneliness. For there is no pleasure greater than in high prosperity to call to mind old misfortunes. But besides giving pleasure, it is considerable help in the practice of virtue.

In addition, Philo gleans two other ethical lessons from Sukkot. First, "that after all the fruits are made perfect, it is our duty to thank God who brought them to perfection and is the source of all good things." And second, "that we should honor equality and hate inequality."

"Spare me," I can hear you saying. The sukkot built by our neighbors take no account of Philo's teachings. Nobody would confuse them with the shacks and shanties of poor people around the world. Nor are all sukkot equal. Between the large, expensive prefabricated ones sold online for as much as $2,000 and their poorer, makeshift cousins, cobbled together from old sheets and piping, sukkot mirror all the inequalities of society at large.

This is true, I confess. But it is also true that an important religious principle underlies the effort to beautify and decorate our seven-day huts. Known in Hebrew as *hiddur mitzvah*, the concept encourages us to embellish and beautify the performance of commandments, to look upon them not just as religious obligations but as spiritual opportunities. Since we make a blessing upon entering the sukkah, we invite visitors to share meals in our sukkah, and our sukkah, according to mystical tradition, is visited by biblical heroes (accompanied, in egalitarian circles, by biblical heroines), we naturally want them to look their best. An aesthetically pleasing sukkah, handsomely constructed and tastefully decorated, helps to make the holiday of Sukkot what tradition says it should be: a time of rejoicing.

AMID THIS REJOICING, however, Sukkot is also an appropriate time to think about "the practice of virtue," the social justice issues that Philo connected to the holiday. The Bible itself mandates that slaves, strangers, orphans, and widows be included in the "Feast of Booths." According to one of the medieval Jewish Bible commentators, we "dwell in booths, as a reminder of those who had no possessions in the wilderness and no houses in which to live."

Through the years, you have become sensitized to this concern for human suffering. Homelessness, hunger, poverty, oppression, cancer—all these causes, and more, have attracted your attention. We are very proud of your well-developed social conscience.

The traditional Hebrew word for many of the activities you have been engaged in is *ḥesed*, often translated as "loving-kindness." Acts of *ḥesed* are selfless acts performed not for the sake of gain or profit but out of consideration for others and a deep sense of love. The world is in large measure sustained by acts of *ḥesed*, according to the Ethics of the Fathers. Each time we assist the poor, visit the sick, comfort the bereaved, bury the dead, and perform other acts of loving-kindness, we serve God and emulate God. One scholar, indeed, characterizes *ḥesed* as "heroic ethics." In a world where so many look out first and foremost for themselves, *ḥesed* is countercultural. It privileges needs, not rights, and relies on the power of love rather than upon the power of might.

Your friends frequently speak of their social justice work as part of what they call *tikkun olam*, mending the world. This term actually dates back to the Jewish mystics of the sixteenth century. According to their complex mythology, tikkun olam aimed to mend the injury suffered by the Godhead when divine light shattered some of the holy vessels meant to contain it, thereby creating evil and disarray in our world. Mending the world back then anticipated the restoration of a more perfect cosmos. It demanded prayer, meditation, and study.

In recent decades, though, the term has taken on a completely different meaning. As used by your friends, it means repairing the condition of the world in the here and now—usually through political and social action. A manifesto by the American Jewish writer and activist Leonard Fein has made the case for tikkun olam powerfully, redefining the concept in contemporary terms:

> *God's world . . . does not work as it was meant to. The story begins with Eden, and goes on through the trials and errors of all the generations since. This exquisitely organic whole, this ecological masterpiece, has been fractured a thousand times, has been scarred and marred and blighted and polluted and bloodied, its beauty transformed, become hideous; it does not work, not as it was meant to, not as it might.*
>
> *We are called to see the beauty through the blemishes, to believe it can be restored, and to feel ourselves implicated in its restoration. We are called to be fixers.*

To be a fixer means to promote social change. Tikkun olam seeks to transform the very basis of society so as to create a more perfect place for human beings to live. Acts of ḥesed, by contrast, ameliorate need. They tend to be more personal and private, focusing on the crises of individuals. To advocate for better and more affordable health care in this country is to engage in tikkun olam. To bring sick people to a clinic or visit them in the hospital is to do an act of ḥesed. The former tend to be more political than the latter, but both draw firmly upon our tradition. And both, in their own way, improve the world that we live in.

SUKKOT ALSO PROMOTES greater appreciation of nature. In Israel, it marks the beginning of the rainy season, which lasts approximately until Passover. On the eighth day of Sukkot, known as Shmini Atzeret (the Eighth day of Assembly), traditional Jews the world over pray for rain. An ancient poem invokes the names of Abraham, Isaac, Jacob, Moses, Aaron, and the twelve tribes, pleading that for the sake of the pious deeds that they performed in biblical days, God should grant the gift of water to us, their descendants.

When I was your age, I thought this was ridiculous. Where we live, after all, there is no rainy season; it rains all year round. Skiers and schoolchildren might pray for snow in winter, but rain? Besides, rain is a meteorological phenomenon governed by science. Why ask God to intervene in nature, I wondered.

Now that I have lived in Israel and experienced a prolonged drought in California, I know better. In places like these with limited water and a long dry season, rain is an absolute blessing. It determines crop yields, reduces the chance of forest fires, and ensures a sufficient supply of water to fill the reservoirs. Years with little or no rain create enormous hardship—even in our world, where water can be shared over long distances and desalination meets some water needs.

In the underdeveloped world, drought can spell catastrophe. Not only do withering crops cause famine and starvation, they also touch off migration, generate competition for scarce water, and frequently spark armed conflict. In my lifetime, this has happened in Africa several times. In antiquity, it happened in the land of Israel as well.

I try and think about all this now when our congregation recites the prayer for rain. I do not know whether our fervent prayer for "the wind to blow and rain to descend" will actually be efficacious. But at least I am more sensitive as to why we should *want* to pray for rain. For millions of people around the world, the words of that ancient poem we recite in our prayer still ring true. Rainfall is the prime determinant of whether the year ahead will be

> *For a blessing and not for a curse*
> *For life and not for death*
> *For abundance and not for famine.*

The prayer for rain draws extra people to our services on Shmini Atzeret, but it is not, I think, the main reason why the crowd every year is abnormally large. Nor do most of those attending appreciate the ancient rabbinic teaching that the eighth day is a special divine gift to the Jewish people, a reward for their dutiful and joyous observance of all the previous fall holidays.

The real draw is the memorial prayers for loved ones, popularly known as *yizkor*, from the Hebrew word "to remember." Recited four times a year (except in most Reform congregations, where it is recited twice a year, on Yom Kippur and Passover), yizkor recalls not only relatives who have passed away but also martyrs, communal leaders, and departed congregants. The custom of reciting these prayers apparently developed during eras of persecution, notably the Crusades and the seventeenth-century attacks on Jews in Eastern Europe. Since then, survivors and descendants alike have prayed that charity and other virtuous deeds performed in the name of the deceased might atone for their unforgiven sins. The goal is to elevate those we pray for to the highest rungs of heaven, so that they may repose, as the prayer puts it, alongside "the other righteous men and women in the Garden of Eden."

You have never really witnessed yizkor. In our synagogue, as in many others, those whose parents are alive step outside during the yizkor service, so as not to give the angel of death any ideas. This effectively creates a congregation of mourners bound together by a common encounter with death's mystery. The words on the page, in

my experience, quickly give way to memories and emo-
tions, as we recall those whom we have loved and lost.

Yizkor has changed in recent years. Nowadays, in
many synagogues, before anybody steps out of the service, we remember, as a community, all those who perished in the ashes of the Holocaust. We likewise
memorialize the thousands who have sacrificed their lives
for the State of Israel as soldiers and civilians. Since the
attacks of September 11, 2001, we recite a prayer recalling the worldwide victims of terror as well.

To me, it always seems especially appropriate to pro-
nounce all these yizkor prayers after seven days in the
sukkah. It is as if the fragile nature of our temporary hut
calls to mind the fragile nature of life itself.

FORTUNATELY, THOUGH, our cycle of fall holidays does
not conclude on this morbid note. The final day of
Sukkot is instead given over to delirious joy. Known as
Simhat Torah, it is a day when we dance and rejoice with
the Torah, complete the annual cycle of reading the
Torah aloud (fittingly enough, the last word of the last
chapter of the book of Deuteronomy is "Israel"), and
commence reading the Torah anew from "In the beginning," the opening chapter of the book of Genesis. The
ritual makes the point that Jewish learning never ends.
The minute we finish reading the last sentence of the
Torah, we circle back and start reading the Torah over
again from the start.

As a child, Simḥat Torah was your favorite among the Jewish fall holidays. You loved the singing, the dancing, and the whole joyous atmosphere of the day (much more fun, you thought, than the somber mood of Rosh Hashanah and Yom Kippur.) You enjoyed the treats that were distributed, the flags that we gave you to carry, and the special children's *aliyah*, when you and your friends could be called up to the Torah and make a blessing. "Why couldn't every holiday be like Simḥat Torah?" you wondered.

We smiled.

Looking back, though, my sense is that Simḥat Torah reminds us of the importance of balance in Jewish life. There is, as the Bible put it, "a time to every purpose": a time for mourning and a time for rejoicing, a time for tikkun olam and a time for Torah, a time to move into a hut and a time to return home. Achieving that balance— among different priorities in Jewish life as well as between Jewish life and workaday life—turns out to be a formidable and never-ending challenge.

As I finish our last preparations for Sukkot, I pray that all of us prove equal to it.

Have a wonderful holiday!

Love,
Abba

ASSIMILATION AND
ANTI-ASSIMILATION

Ḥanukkah

Dear Leah,

Sorry to have been out of touch for so long. Once the fall holidays ended, I found myself overwhelmed with work deadlines and travel obligations. I have been laboring day and night for weeks. The Jewish calendar as a whole, I think, promotes something of a feast-or-famine cycle. Earlier in the fall, during Rosh Hashanah, Yom Kippur, and Sukkot, I wondered when I would ever get any work done. Now, just two months later, I feel like I desperately need a holiday!

Fortunately, the ancient rabbis created one—though the holiday they established lacks the status of the major biblical festivals. Technically speaking it is only a half-holiday, so there are no prohibitions on work and no lengthy religious services to attend. In fact, the holiday's major ritual could scarcely be simpler: light candles at dusk, one more each evening, for eight successive nights.

Nevertheless, and mostly because of when it occurs in juxtaposition with the civil calendar, the holiday is among the best known and most beloved of all the Jewish holidays. Its name is Ḥanukkah.

Ḥanukkah means "dedication." Almost twenty-two hundred years ago, Judah Maccabee and his followers liberated the ancient temple in Jerusalem from the Syrian Greeks and rededicated it to the God of Israel. They celebrated for eight days, recalling the eight-day celebration of the temple's original dedication. According to tradition, a single cruse of temple oil, sufficient for but one day of illumination, miraculously kept the temple candelabrum burning for eight days straight.

The villain of the Ḥanukkah story is Antiochus IV Epiphanes, the Seleucid King of the Hellenistic Syrian Kingdom. He promoted Hellenization, expecting Jews to abandon their own religion and culture for that of the Greeks. His goal was to promote religious homogeneity within his kingdom: "All should be one people . . . each should give up his [individual] customs." To this end, he established the cult of Zeus as the state religion, outlawed circumcision and the Sabbath, defiled and despoiled the temple, and banned the practice of Judaism altogether.

Many Jews, we know, adopted the ways of the Greeks. They assumed Greek names, followed Greek practices, and bowed down to Greek gods. But Mattathias, the father of Judah Maccabee, resisted. His words, recorded in the book of Maccabees, echo through the ages as a testament to religious liberty and minority group rights:

> *Even if all the nations that live under the rule of the king obey him, and have chosen to do his commandments, departing each one from the religion of his fathers, yet I and my sons and my brothers will live by the covenant of our fathers. Far be it from us to desert the law and the ordinances. We will not obey the king's words by turning aside from our religion to the right hand or to the left. . . . Let every one who is zealous for the law and supports the covenant come out with me!*

Mattathias's declaration of independence fueled the revolt that defeated the Syrian Greeks. It resulted in renewed Jewish autonomy and the rededication of the Temple. More broadly, it kept the Jewish religion alive and contributed to the spread of monotheism throughout Western civilization.

I can almost see your eyes rolling. That is not why you and your friends look forward to Ḥanukkah! You like the presents that are now a central feature of the holiday. You like the family gatherings, the candles, the songs, the jelly donuts, and the potato pancakes that we call latkes (these oily foods supposedly recall the miracle of the oil that lasted for eight days). While most Americans celebrate Christmas for one day, we observe Ḥanukkah for eight!

Truth be told, the proximity of Christmas to Hanukkah explains much of the holiday's popularity. In the colonial period, when Christmas was actually outlawed in Massachusetts, Hanukkah played a very minor role in Jewish life; it had nothing to do with gift giving at all. Once Christmas grew in popularity and became a national holiday, however, Hanukkah was revived and magnified. By now, for many of your friends, Hanukkah has less to do with history and continuity than with its being the Jewish answer to Christmas.

Christmas! When you were growing up, it was by far the hardest day of the year for us. More than any other day of the year, it set you apart from your non-Jewish friends. Explaining why we had no Christmas tree, no Christmas decorations, no Christmas dinner—in fact, no Christmas at all—forced you to confront what it meant to be a member of a minority faith. America might look upon Christmas as a national holiday, but for Jews, we explained, it was our neighbors' holiday; we celebrate Hanukkah.

Hanukkah did not always cooperate. One year, owing to the vagaries of the lunar calendar, it actually coincided with Thanksgiving. But even in those years when Christmas and Hanukkah coincided perfectly, we knew that treating Hanukkah as if it were the "Jewish Christmas" was something of a fraud. Hanukkah, after all, celebrates those who *resisted* pressures to conform religiously and culturally. It is, in a sense, the holiday of anti-assimilation.

It promotes the right to be different. Far from being the Jewish Christmas, Ḥanukkah should really be celebrated as the Jewish *anti*-Christmas.

"But you go to Christmas parties," you might protest. "Besides, in a country that associates Christmas with 'peace on earth and goodwill to all,' why should Jews want to play Scrooge and stand apart?"

There is much truth in this. I do join colleagues at Christmas parties. And I certainly uphold the virtues of peace on earth and goodwill to all. But, for me, going to a Christmas party is like going to a friend's birthday party. The party is for the honoree; I am only a guest.

As a Jew, it comes naturally for me to feel both part of the larger society in which I live and simultaneously apart from it. I know that other minority groups in America— Armenians, Greeks, Muslims, and certainly African Americans—feel much the same way. In approaching Christmas and Ḥanukkah, I try to balance these contradictory feelings. I wish my Christian neighbors a Merry Christmas and rejoice in the dazzling beauty of the Christmas decorations on the street. But I take care never to make Christmas my holiday. My holiday is Ḥanukkah.

We know people who celebrate both Christmas and Ḥanukkah, and you once asked me why we could not do likewise. Now, a student of mine has taught me a new word—Chrismukkah—which a television character with a Jewish father and a Protestant mother claims to have invented as a way of merging his two faiths. The idea is to borrow favorite traditions from both December holidays and mix them together. Rather than choosing between Christmas and Ḥanukkah, one can pretend to have both at once.

For me, at least, this idea holds no appeal. I prefer authentic religious traditions that link us to our ancestors and to those who share our faith around the world. Most Christians I know feel the same way about their traditions. It is absolutely fine to admire other peoples' traditions from afar, but to filch those traditions, secularize them, and then mix them with traditions from wholly different faiths strikes me as ill-mannered and irresponsible. A little bit of this and a little bit of that may be fine for a stew, but sacred family rituals, to my mind, should be built upon more solid foundations.

MOST OF THE PEOPLE I KNOW who seek to forge a Christmas-Ḥanukkah hybrid are intermarried. One parent warmly recalls lighting Ḥanukkah candles; the other fondly remembers presents under the tree on Christmas morning. Grandparents on both sides beckon: offering beautiful Christmas presents at one house, magnificent Ḥanukkah ones at the other. Faced with this December dilemma, parents struggle. Which holiday should we choose, they wonder. Can't we find some way for our children to celebrate both?

The December dilemma is, essentially, insoluble, but I am glad for you to think about the complexities of intermarriage at this time of the year. Now that you are dating, you need to make mature decisions concerning this oh-so-sensitive subject. Can you answer each of the following questions comfortably? I hope that you have given the matter lots of thought.

- Are you willing to date a non-Jew?
- Would you marry someone not Jewish, or would you insist that that person convert to Judaism first?
- If you would marry a non-Jew, what decision would you make concerning children? Would they absolutely have to be raised Jewish, or is that subject to negotiation?

Your grandparents, as you know, never faced any of these daunting questions. It was self-evident to them that they needed to marry within the faith. That is what most people did at that time, Jews and non-Jews alike. "Birds of a feather flock together," the old adage went. For the most part, in those days, Jews married Jews, Protestants married Protestants, and Catholics married Catholics.

Nowadays, America has changed. Marriages across religious lines have become commonplace. Protestants, Catholics, even Greek Orthodox Americans regularly "marry out." No surprise, then, that people your age champion the ideal of robust choice in marriage. In our country, where the democratic ideal prevails, everybody properly feels free to marry everybody else. Love, we are taught, conquers all.

Traditional Judaism, of course, promotes a very different view. Some twenty-five hundred years ago, in the days of Ezra and Nehemiah, Jews pledged that "we will not give our daughters in marriage to the peoples of the land or take their daughters for our sons." At least since that time, endogamy—in-group marriage—has been a preeminent value among Jews. This has facilitated the transmission of faith and culture across the generations and has kept Jews from disappearing into the mainstream. Intermarriage was seen as undermining this value and threatening the character and preservation of the Jewish group. As a result, the taboo against intermarriage became one of the strongest and most deeply rooted taboos in Jewish life.

So which will you uphold: the modern American value or the traditional Jewish one?

This, I know, is no easy question. Issues that force us to choose between American and Jewish values—such as Christmas or Ḥanukkah, playing in the World Series or observing Yom Kippur—never are easy. They tend to be the most agonizing dilemmas that we face.

What makes the issue particularly difficult, in this case, is that so much is at stake. With close to half of all American Jews intermarrying these days, the Jewish community in the United States could literally disappear.

This has happened before. Remember the famous Lost Ten Tribes? The ten northern tribes of the Kingdom of Israel were deported to Mesopotamia by the Assyrians in the eighth century BCE. Through the years, many fantastic tales have been invented to explain their disappearance. We now know, however, that the vast majority of the deported Jews struck roots in Mesopotamia and settled down. Some of them rose to high economic and social positions, and a few came to occupy prestigious posts within the Assyrian government. As a group, they assimilated, intermarried, became absorbed into the local milieu—and, over time, disappeared as Jews.

The same thing happened, more recently, on the Caribbean island of Jamaica. There has been a Jewish community in Jamaica since the seventeenth century, and in 1881 there were some twenty-five hundred Jews there, about 18 percent of that community's white population. Large numbers of Jews intermarried, however, and the community withered. Today, Jamaica boasts many citizens with Jewish ancestors and Jewish-sounding last names, but only about three hundred of them are still Jewish.

Among intermarried people we know here in the United States, different patterns prevail. Several of them have influenced their partners to convert to Judaism. In one case, the conversion took place before the wedding, but in another the conversion took place many years later, after the couple had children. Their families are both fully committed to Judaism and represent a net gain for our "endangered species."

Others, however, made a different decision. The husband of one of our intermarried friends, though not deeply religious as a Methodist, remains close to his parents; he could not bring himself to convert from the faith in which they had raised him. He did agree that his children would be brought up exclusively as Jews. His youngest child told me that he likes being Jewish but is glad that he still gets to observe Christmas and Easter with his grandparents. I did not ask him whether he himself would want to marry a Jew when he grows up.

For the most part, though, the intermarried people we know have abandoned Judaism. Some are Christian or Buddhist. Many profess no religion. A few try to raise children in two religions (generally a disaster, especially when those religions expect exclusive attachments). Others gravitate to what they see as a "compromise" religion, like Unitarianism or Messianic Judaism—both of which, from a Jewish point of view, are not Jewish at all since they recognize Jesus as the messiah. At least 1.5 million people in the United States have Jewish grandparents but are not Jewish themselves. Most of them are the products of intermarriages. Given the estimate of 5.3 million Jews currently in the United States, that suggests that, but for intermarriage, the Jewish community might be a lot larger.

Ironically, the very qualities that have made American society so desirable to us as Jews—its tolerance, its liberal tradition, and its emphasis on individual rights and privileges—are the same qualities that facilitate marriage across ethnic and religious lines. Indeed, the more we win acceptance as equal and desirable fellow citizens, the more likely we are to lose our distinctive identity through marital assimilation.

It takes conscious effort to preserve endangered religious minorities in our country. Jews, Greek Orthodox, Armenians, Zoroastrians—all fear for their long-term survival in the American melting pot. This helps to explain why the issue of intermarriage is so emotionally fraught in our community. Given our small numbers, the issue may literally mean life or death for our people's surviving remnant.

So please think about this as you watch the candles slowly burn down on Ḥanukkah. And think about Mattathias and Judah Maccabee. By dissenting from the mainstream, they assured the continued existence of the Jewish religion. What will your legacy be?

Whatever you choose, your mother and I will always love you.

Happy Ḥanukkah!

Love,
Abba

GOING GREEN

Tu bi-Shevat

Dear Leah,

Happy New Year—again!

No, it is not Rosh Hashanah, and I am not going out of my mind. Today, according to the Jewish calendar, is the fifteenth day of the month of Shevat, known in Hebrew as Tu bi-Shevat. It is the new year for trees, the beginning of spring.

The Talmud records that there are four new years celebrated annually: one for kings, one for tithing animals, one for years (Rosh Hashanah), and one for trees. Today we celebrate only the last two. In terms of trees, fruits that blossom after Tu bi-Shevat, by which time the bulk of the rain in Israel has fallen, belong to a new agricultural year.

Where we live, of course, mounds of snow usually cover the trees on Tu bi-Shevat. There is no hope of seeing trees blossom. One year, though, I managed to be in

Israel on Tu bi-Shevat. There, lo and behold, the almond trees were gloriously in bloom.

Tu bi-Shevat is a minor Jewish holiday. Nobody takes time off from work or school to celebrate it. No special prayers are recited in the synagogue. In much of the Jewish world, I am sorry to say, the day goes unmarked completely.

When I was growing up, we raised money to plant trees in Israel on Tu bi-Shevat, turning the day into a kind of Jewish Arbor Day. Next time you visit one of the beautiful forests that now dot the Israeli landscape, think of all the little saplings that my classmates and I dutifully sponsored. (I still have some of the old certificates.) How proud we were to help make the desert bloom!

And bloom it did. I read recently that Israel is the only country in the entire world that has more trees today than it had in 1900. Renewing the land, making it green and lush and beautiful, was a high priority for the Jewish pioneers who returned to the land of Israel. In a famous poem, the Israeli poet Shin Shalom captures the belief that when the desert fully blooms, the Messiah will appear:

> *On the fifteenth of Shevat,*
> *When the spring comes,*
> *An angel descends, ledger in hand.*
> *And enters each bud, each twig, each tree*
> *And all our garden flowers.*

From town to town, from village to village
He makes his winged way.
Searching the valleys, inspecting the hills,
Flying over the desert.
And returns to heaven.
And when the ledger will be full
Of trees and blossoms and shrubs,
When the desert is turned into a meadow
And all our land is a watered garden,
The Messiah will appear.

The poet's linking of Tu bi-Shevat to the coming of the messiah recalls the fact that it was the community of mystics—the same kabbalists who brought us the all-night study session, Tikkun Leil Shavuot, that I wrote you about in an earlier letter—who also revitalized Tu bi-Shevat. In sixteenth-century Safed, these kabbalists created a seder, loosely modeled on its Passover counterpart, to mark Tu bi-Shevat ceremonially and recall the Garden of Eden.

As part of the seder, the kabbalists recited ancient texts dealing with trees and their produce. My favorite compares the Jewish people to a pile of walnuts. "If one walnut is removed, each and every nut in the pile is shaken and disturbed. So too, when a single Jew is in distress, every other Jew is shaken." Participants in the seder also meditated, consumed fifteen different kinds of fruits and nuts from the land of Israel, and downed four glasses of wine, beginning with white wine and slowly darkening to red. Every part of their seder was deeply symbolic, reflecting the kabbalists' belief that the entire cosmos is mystically interlinked. Just as Tu bi-Shevat marks the renewal of trees, so the kabbalists looked forward to the renewal and redemption of the Jewish people and of humanity as a whole.

TODAY, TU BI-SHEVAT has found new life in our community as a day for environmental awareness. This may surprise you. I do not recall that Jewish beliefs concerning the environment played much role in your Jewish education. But our tradition is fabulously rich. As interest in the environment has grown, Jewish teachings about these issues have been rediscovered.

Remember the creation story in the book of Genesis? One of my students was greatly disturbed by the notion that God gave humanity the right to "fill the earth and master it." Giving human beings so much power over the environment, she argued, paved the way for ecological disaster. Mastering the earth, to her, meant destroying it.

Fortunately, modern scholars understand the biblical idiom differently. The Bible, they insist, made human being the *stewards* of the earth, not its master at all. Our job, as a consequence, is to preserve the natural order and not to subvert it. A wonderful old rabbinic legend that I learned last Tu bi-Shevat underscores this very message:

The Holy Blessed One took the first human, and passing before all the trees of the Garden of Eden, said, "See my works, how fine and excellent they are! All that I created, I created for you. Reflect on this, and do not corrupt or desolate my world; for if you do, there will be no one to repair it after you."

My favorite biblical teaching concerning trees and the environment is the principle of *bal tashḥit*—"do not destroy." The book of Deuteronomy forbids the destruction of fruit trees in wartime ("You may eat of them, but you must not cut them down"). Later rabbis extended this principle to apply to any kind of needless waste. "Whoever breaks vessels, tears clothes, demolishes a building, stops up a fountain or wastes food, in a destructive way, offends against the law of 'thou shalt not destroy,'" Maimonides wrote. Another rabbi insisted that the truly pious "never destroy even a grain of mustard, and are upset at any destruction they see." In a wasteful society like ours, these words provide a wonderful religious justification for recycling!

Judaism, of course, does not speak with one voice concerning attitudes toward nature. Rabbi Joseph in the Ethics of the Fathers, for example, teaches that a person who interrupts the study of the Torah to exclaim "how beautiful is this tree, how beautiful is this field," is called to account as if he or she had committed a mortal sin. My teacher, years ago, took this to mean that studying Torah is vastly more important than admiring nature. A contemporary Jewish writer, Cynthia Ozick, warns that admiring nature too much can lead to paganism.

These days, though, I see Rabbi Joseph's teaching explained in a very different way. "It is not the expression of praise for the beauty of God's creation that is condemned here," a popular commentary declares, "but the interruption of one's studies." Whatever the case, you will be relieved to hear that a far less ambiguous view concerning the beauty of nature was expressed by Rabbi Abraham, the son of Moses Maimonides. "In order to serve God, one needs access to the enjoyment of the beauties of nature," he wrote. "These are essential to the spiritual development of even the holiest people."

Air pollution, water pollution, even noise pollution—all of these, it turns out, are prohibited in rabbinic sources. The rabbis also discuss the importance of preserving green spaces surrounding cities. One scholar in thirteenth-century Barcelona went so far as to ban what we would call environmental waivers, construction projects that receive one-time exemptions from environmental ordinances. Laws passed to protect the quality of community life, he ruled, could not subsequently be forgone. Nothing in Judaism requires the sacrifice of environmental quality on the altar of economic growth.

Perhaps because our tradition is so rich with environmental pronouncements and because almost nobody knows about them, a new organization was founded a few years back called the Coalition on the Environment and Jewish Life (COEJL). Its founders span the full spectrum of Jewish religious and political life—meaning that they disagree about almost everything important. Amazingly, though, they managed to unite, according to their public statement, "in deep concern that the quality of human life and the earth we inhabit are in danger, afflicted by rapidly increasing ecological threats." Their mission statement helps to explain why Tu bi-Shevat has taken on new significance in our day and why environmentalism is now such a vital Jewish issue:

> *For Jews, the environmental crisis is a religious challenge. As heirs to a tradition of stewardship that goes back to Genesis and that teaches us to be partners in the ongoing work of Creation, we cannot accept the escalating destruction of our environment and its effect on human health and livelihood. Where we are despoiling our air, land, and water, it is our sacred duty as Jews to acknowledge our God-given responsibility and take action to alleviate environmental degradation and the pain and suffering that it causes. We must reaffirm and bequeath the tradition we have inherited which calls upon us to safeguard humanity's home.*

This year, on Tu bi-Shevat, you may want to learn more about the Coalition on the Environment and Jewish Life and the work of other Jewish organizations involved in environmental action. Think about becoming involved in their activities.

I cannot imagine a better way to start off the new year for trees.

Love,
Abba

CONTINUITY AND HAPPINESS

Purim

Dear Leah,

It's topsy-turvy day, a celebration of Jewish deliverance from extermination twenty-five hundred years ago.

You never heard of a Jewish holiday named "Topsy-Turvy"? The biblical book of Esther reports that the world turned upside-down on the wicked Haman, the vizier of Persia. His genocidal plan was to hang "Mordecai the Jew" and wipe out the Jewish people as a whole, who refused to bow down to him. Casting lots, he selected the thirteenth of Adar "to destroy, massacre, and exterminate all the Jews, young and old, children and women on a single day . . . and to plunder their possessions."

The plan, however, was successfully thwarted. Thanks to behind-the-scenes work by the pious Mordecai and some clever machinations by his niece, Persia's beautiful Queen Esther (herself a secret Jew), Haman's designs were dramatically exposed at a royal party. King Xerxes, named Ahasuerus in the Bible, ordered Haman hanged on the very tree that he had prepared for Mordecai's hanging; the rest of Haman's family was likewise wiped out. The Jews, meanwhile, were saved, and Mordecai replaced Haman as Persia's vizier.

Since then, Jews have celebrated a rollicking holiday named Purim (meaning "lots") to mark this miraculous turn in their fortunes. The day is characterized by much merrymaking, as well as a spirit of inversion.

I am celebrating Purim in Brooklyn this year. Here, in the fervently Orthodox Jewish sections of Williamsburg and Boro Park, the day is marked with masks and merriment and (heavy) drinking. For twenty-four hours, the standard rules of order are flouted. Tomfoolery reins supreme, and much that would be prohibited on all other days of the year—from public intoxication to cross-dressing—is permitted.

Purim is one of the most unusual holidays of the Jewish year. The events it commemorates took place not in Israel but in the diaspora—in Persia. The traditional Purim story reads like an Oriental romance, complete with palace intrigue, drinking banquets, low comedy, even bawdy language ("Does he mean," cried the king, "to ravish the queen in my own palace?"). God and religious observance go practically unmentioned in the biblical story. Human beings—Mordecai, and especially Queen Esther—save the day, ensuring the triumph of good over evil.

The result is the very first Jewish festival not mentioned in the Torah and not focused on the land of Israel. It is a day set aside for "feasting and merrymaking . . . for sending gifts to one another and presents to the poor." The Talmud goes so far as to encourage Jews to get so drunk that they cannot distinguish between "Cursed be Haman" and "Blessed be Mordecai."

Last night, in honor of Purim, I attended a service here where the book of Esther was chanted, as it is throughout the world, from a large hand-written scroll, called a *megillah*. It was folded up by the reader so that it looked somewhat like a letter. Each time the name of the wicked Haman was read out, the audience made an enormous ruckus with noisemakers, the banging of feet, hisses, and the like. The reader injected a good deal of humor into his chanting, using different voices for different characters (some of them in falsetto). It made for good theater, with lots of audience participation.

Later, there was a Purim party at one of the many Jewish schools here. The carnival atmosphere reflected the same spirit of inversion that I noticed earlier. The students ran the show and poked fun at their teachers and administrators. In one of the skits, a few boys played girls' parts. In another skit, they dressed up as irreligious Jews (a caricature, I thought). In still a third, they impersonated Arab terrorists. An anthropologist could have had a field day analyzing all these skits. Their humor

exposes the divisions, tensions, and insecurities of contemporary Jewish life.

THIS MORNING, I attended a different Brooklyn synagogue. There I listened to the traditional reading from
the Torah for Purim, which prefigures the book of Esther.
It is the story of the Israelites' war with the Amalekites,
and it always makes me somewhat uncomfortable.

The Amalekites, according to the book of Exodus,
waged a surprise attack against the "famished and weary"
Israelites marching in the desert and murdered many in-
nocents. During the course of the ensuing difficult battle,
Moses raised his arms heavenward, and the Amalekites
were repulsed. God thereupon promised retribution for
the Amalekites' perfidy: "I will utterly blot out the memory of Amalek from under heaven. . . . The Lord will be at
war with Amalek throughout the ages." According to Jewish tradition, all antisemites, Haman in particular, descend,
genetically or spiritually, from the Amalekites, and the
memory of all of them will ultimately be "blotted out."

This is a troubling text in many ways. How can God
mandate the destruction of an entire people, even if they
did act wickedly? How can we today still be commanded
to "blot out the memory of Amalek"? How, if all contemporary enemies of Israel are descendants of Amalek, are
we supposed to treat them?

The rabbis, as usual, put forward a wide range of responses. Some explain that the last Amalekites were wiped

out back in the days of King Saul, the first king of ancient Israel. Others insist that, yes, even today each of us is responsible for wiping out the descendants of Amalek—but only genetic descendants, and we do not know how to find them. Still others maintain that our job is simply to remember and recount the story as a lesson that Jews survive and their enemies do not.

Personally, I have no interest in exterminating anybody and would have no idea how to recognize an Amalekite (much less blot out his memory) even if I met one. But at a time when we Jews once again face formidable enemies who would love nothing more than to exterminate us, this powerful reminder of Jewish survival amid adversity seems to me wonderfully timely.

"Survival for what?" you may immediately complain. "Shouldn't we Jews do more than just outwit and outlive our enemies?"

True enough! Survival is only a first step. Maybe that's why we send gifts to our friends on Purim and also presents to the poor. By establishing caring communities, helping one another, and taking responsibility for the disadvantaged in our midst, we signify that we seek not only to survive but to build a better and more caring world as well.

Let's not take our survival for granted, however. Who would have believed, after all, that we could last two thousand years as a small minority exiled from its homeland? Who would have believed that we could survive massacres and expulsions and even gas chambers? That we could survive communism, a political system that banned Jewish religious practices and the study of Jewish culture? For that matter, who would have believed that we could survive freedom, with all its seductive temptations to assimilate, intermarry, and amalgamate into the mainstream? When you think about it, our survival, however precarious, is absolutely astonishing.

How to explain it? What is the secret of Jewish continuity?

"God," many people I know will unhesitatingly reply. In the story of Purim and in every subsequent example of miraculous deliverance, traditional Jews see the hand of God maneuvering behind the scenes.

"Community," others will counter. Jews flourish in close-knit communities where they can live, marry, and raise children among those who share their own faith and customs. The supportive web of community, more than anything else, promotes Jewish continuity, especially when adversity strikes.

"Prophets of gloom and doom," a more cynical historian may suggest. Perennial warnings that Jews are endangered, that Jews are assimilating, that Jews will die out, and so forth, serve a vital function. By fomenting fear, however exaggerated, they rouse the community to action, mobilizing its energy in response to the dangers that loom. By predicting that Jews will *not* survive, doleful prophets help to ensure that they *will*.

"Change," more progressive Jews may exclaim. More often than not, when Jewish continuity is threatened, new historical conditions create new movements, new emphases, new paradigms—discontinuities that promote continuity. Innovations such as the movement to create a Jewish state, the Jewish day school movement, and, in our day, the Jewish women's movement, all are examples of this paradox. They demonstrate the power of change in Jewish life.

"Individual effort," still others may insist. Just as Mordecai and Esther figured out how to subvert Haman's plans, countless other Jews—young and old, women and men alike—have changed the course of history and ensured that Jews live on. We Jews are not mere objects of history, buffeted by outside forces; we actually *shape* history. Each of us can make a difference. Survival today and the future of the Jewish people tomorrow depend upon the work of individual Jews.

I love each of these answers and see no need to choose among them. All of them, in their own way, ring true. Together they seem to me to explain a great deal about Jewish survival. Just hearing them fills me up with optimism and joy.

Now, IN THAT intoxicatingly happy state of mind, I am off to a great Purim feast. Like everything else on this topsy-turvy day, it seems slightly askew. The meal begins surprisingly early. It must start before sunset (when

Purim ends) but will continue, I am told, far into the night. Food, I know, will be plentiful—nothing unusual there—but alcohol will flow plentifully too, more than on any other day in the Jewish year. The meal even promises entertainment in the form of a play, known as a *Purimshpil*, complete with musical accompaniment. Some scholars believe that the entire Jewish theatrical tradition has its origin in Purim plays like this; they date back centuries. In the past, such plays dramatized (usually with up-to-date details and a good deal of slapstick humor) the Purim story and other biblical narratives, but today they are as likely to draw upon history, folklore, and contemporary culture. I wonder what the play will be about this year?

I EXPECT TO GET BACK too late tonight to write to you about the great feast. Tomorrow, when I wake up and my head clears, I will recognize with a start that Passover is but one month away. Your Mother, knowing how time flies, will insist that I rush home at once to begin cleaning and preparing.

So let me close now with this thought: The Jewish future rests in your hands. Will you carry forward our traditions, woven into the very fabric of the Jewish year? Will you work, as a Jew, to improve the world? Will you remember that we are a small and endangered people and act accordingly? Will you study Judaism, practice

Judaism, and then transmit Judaism, someday, to your own children?

These are not new questions, I know, but I pose them again for a reason. As the old Danish proverb puts it, "Better to ask twice than to lose your way once."

See you next month at the seder!

Love,
Abba

FOR FURTHER READING

The *Encyclopaedia Judaica* (1972, 2nd ed. 2007) is the first source for up-to-date articles on Jewish topics. In addition to the print version, it is now available online at universities and public libraries. The older *Jewish Encyclopedia*, completed in 1906, is available free at Jewish Encyclopedia.com and is very easy to navigate. Don't bother looking there for articles on the Holocaust or the modern State of Israel, but for information prior to the twentieth century it is highly reliable.

Wonderful brief articles on a wide range of subjects may be found in two comprehensive books: Joseph Telushkin, *Jewish Literacy: The Most Important Things to Know About the Jewish Religion, Its People, and Its History* (1991), and Louis Jacobs, *The Jewish Religion: A Companion* (1995). An online edition of the latter is available for a fee. For critical concepts, movements, and beliefs in Judaism, see Arthur A. Cohen and Paul Mendes-Flohr, *Contemporary Jewish Religious Thought* (1987). Another, somewhat more basic source for reliable information concerning Jewish topics is MyJewishLearning.com.

With sections on culture, daily life and practice, holidays, history and community, life cycle, ideas and beliefs, texts, and special topics (like the Holocaust, Israel, and women in Judaism), as well as lots of helpful links, it is a readily accessible portal for online inquiries.

Philip Goodman edited seven wide-ranging Jewish holiday anthologies published by the Jewish Publication Society (JPS): *The Passover Anthology* (1961), *The Shavuot Anthology* (1975), *The Rosh Hashanah Anthology* (1970), *The Yom Kippur Anthology* (1971), *The Sukkot and Simḥat Torah Anthology* (1973), *The Ḥanukkah Anthology* (1976), and *The Purim Anthology* (1949). The books include material from a broad variety of texts and all the major Jewish religious movements. More recently, Paul Steinberg has produced a three-volume holiday anthology, also published by JPS, entitled *Celebrating the Jewish Year* (2007–2008). One volume covers the fall holidays, one the winter holidays, and the third the spring and summer holidays. *Celebrating the Jewish Holidays*, edited by Steven J. Rubin (2003), is a one-volume anthology of poems, stories, and essays for the Sabbath and five Jewish holidays.

Guides to the Jewish festivals abound. *The Jewish Festivals: History and Observance* by Hayyim Schauss (1938) provides a brief reliable account. *The Book of Our Heritage: The Jewish Year and Its Days of Significance* by Eliyahu Kitov (3 vols., 1970) is longer and more Orthodox in orientation. *Festivals of the Jewish Year: A Modern*

Interpretation and Guide by Theodor H. Gaster (1953) is beautifully written and draws many insights from comparative religion and anthropology. In *Seasons of Our Joy: A Handbook of Jewish Festivals* (1982), Arthur I. Waskow sets the "mood" for particular holidays and offers creative interpretations and innovative customs in addition to more traditional ones. Irving Greenberg's *The Jewish Way: Living the Holidays* (1988) is comprehensive and unfailingly thoughtful. *The [First] Jewish Catalog*, edited by Richard Siegel, Michael Strassfeld, and Sharon Strassfeld (1973), served as the "Bible" for young countercultural Jews a generation ago, and bills itself as a "do-it-yourself kit" for those seeking to become personally involved in Jewish life. Scott-Martin Kosofsky's handsomely designed *The Book of Customs: A Complete Handbook for the Jewish Year* (2004), updates a Yiddish classic, providing readers with charming insights into the rituals, liturgies, and texts that mark the Jewish year.

The haggadah is the key to understanding the holiday of Passover. In *Haggadah and History: A Panorama in Facsimile of Five Centuries of the Printed Haggadah* (1975), Yosef H. Yerushalmi shows how Jews in different ages and places related the traditional text of the haggadah to their own situations. *My People's Passover Haggadah: Traditional Texts, Modern Commentaries*, edited by Lawrence A. Hoffman and David Arnow (2 vols., 2008), supplies abundant background from multiple perspectives. Jonathan Sacks introduces the major themes of the Haggadah and explains its larger significance in *Rabbi Jonathan Sacks's Haggadah: Hebrew and English Text with New Essays and Commentary* (2006). In *American Heritage Haggadah: The Passover Experience* (1992), editor David Geffen underscores the relationship between Passover and the American Jewish experience.

In "The Mimuna and the Minority Status of Moroccan Jews," *Ethnology* 17, no. 1 (January 1978), pp. 75–87, Harvey E. Goldberg explains key aspects of the Maimuna holiday celebrated by Moroccan Jews and provides other sources. For background on Moroccan Jewry, consult Daniel J. Schroeter, *The Sultan's Jews: Morocco and the Sephardi World* (2002); and Reeva S. Simon, Michael M. Laskier, and Sara Reguer, eds., *The Jews of the Middle East and North Africa in Modern Times* (2003).

Thousands of books now deal with various aspects of the Shoah. The most comprehensive and reliable is the award-winning two-volume set by Saul Friedländer covering *The Years of Persecution, 1933–1939* (1998) and *The Years of Extermination, 1939–1945* (2007). The best of the one-volume surveys is Len Yahil, Ina Friedman, and Haya Galai, *The Holocaust: The Fate of European Jewry 1932–1945* (1991). For Yom Hashoah, see Marcia Sachs Littell, ed., *Liturgies on the Holocaust: An Interfaith Anthology* (1986); Elie Wiesel and Albert H. Friedlander, *The Six Days of Destruction: Meditations Toward Hope* (1988); Abba Kovner, *Scrolls of Testimony* (2001); and *Megilat ha-Sho'ah—The Shoah Scroll: A Holocaust Liturgy* (2004).

Israel, too, has been the subject of innumerable books. The best one-volume history in English is Howard M. Sachar's definitive *A History of Israel from the Rise of Zionism to Our Time* (2007). Itamar Rabinovich and Jehuda Reinharz provide a brilliant collection of primary sources in *Israel in the Middle East: Documents and Readings on Society, Politics, and Foreign Relations, Pre-1948 to the Present* (2008). In *Six Days of War: June 1967 and the Making of the Modern Middle East* (2002), Michael B. Oren vividly recreates the conflict that transformed so much of Israel's history. *Jews in Israel: Contemporary Social and Cultural Patterns*, edited by Uzi Rebhun and Chaim I. Waxman (2004), looks beyond the Arab-Israeli conflict to examine the challenges and contradictions of modern Israel. In *The Case for Israel* (2003), Alan Dershowitz effectively rebuts critics of Israel's very existence.

To learn more about the Torah, which, according to Jewish tradition, was given to the children of Israel on the day now celebrated as Shavuot, one cannot do better than to study the text of the Torah. There is no shortage of available resources. Each of the three major movements of Judaism has its own one-volume English-language Torah commentary. Reform Jews favor W. Gunther Plaut, *The Torah : A Modern Commentary* (1981, 2005); Conservative Jews prefer *Etz Hayim: Torah and Commentary* (2001); and Orthodox Jews tend to use *The Chumash: The ArtScroll Series Stone Edition* (1993). Other recent translations and commentaries include Everett Fox, *The Five Books of Moses* (1995); and Robert Alter, *The Five Books of Moses: A Translation With Commentary* (2004). Nahum M. Sarna edited the five-volume *JPS Torah Commentary* (1996) for those seeking to probe deeper using modern tools. ArtScroll Press has produced translations of many of the traditional medieval Torah commentaries. *The Jewish Study Bible*, edited by Adele Berlin and Marc Zvi Brettler, (2004) covers all thirty-nine books of the Hebrew Bible, with translation, commentaries, scholarly essays, tables, charts, and maps.

One way to appreciate Tishah be-Av is to study its liturgy, particularly the *kinot* (dirges) that commemorate different Jewish tragedies. For translations, see Abraham Rosenfeld, *The Authorised Kinot for the Ninth of Av* (1979); and Chaim Feuer and Avie Gold, *Kinnos / Tishah B'av Service* (1992). For commentary, see Joseph D. Soloveitchik, *The Lord Is Righteous in All His Ways: Reflections on the Tish'ah be-Av Kinot*, edited by Jacob J. Schacter (2006). More broadly, on the history of antisemitism, see Leon Poliakov, *The History of Anti-Semitism* (4 vols., 1965); Shmuel Almog, ed., *Antisemitism Through the Ages* (1988); and Walter Laqueur, *The Changing Face of Antisemitism from Ancient Times to the Present Day* (2006). Leonard Dinnerstein has produced the best one-volume narrative history, *Antisemitism in America* (1994). Dennis Prager and Joseph Telushkin take up the question *Why the Jews? The Reason for Antisemitism* (1983). Kenneth

Stern brings the story up-to-date in *Antisemitism Today: How It Is the Same, How It Is Different, and How to Fight It* (2006).

Those seeking love on Tu be-Av may want to read one of the many Jewish guides to the subject, such as Maurice Lamm, *The Jewish Way in Love and Marriage* (1991); Anita Diamant, *The New Jewish Wedding* (1985); Michael Gold, *God, Love, Sex, and Family: A Rabbi's Guide for Building Relationships That Last* (1998); or Shmuley Boteach, *Kosher Sex: A Recipe for Passion and Intimacy* (1999). For fine collections of articles, see Philip Goodman and Hanna Goodman, *The Jewish Marriage Anthology* (1965); Carol Diament, ed., *Jewish Marital Status* (1989); and Michael J. Broyde and Michael Ausubel, *Marriage, Sex, and Family in Judaism* (2005). Much can be learned about Jewish demographics around the world from the annual volumes of the *American Jewish Year Book*. Past volumes (106 of them!) are available online at AJCArchives.org.

The Rosh Hashanah liturgy, contained in a high holiday prayer book known as the *mahzor*, serves as an excellent introduction to the themes of the high holidays. Each of the major movements has published its own liturgy: Reform, *Gates of Repentance: The New Union Prayerbook for the Days of Awe* (1996); Reconstructionist, *Kol Haneshamah Prayerbook for the Days of Awe* (1999); Conservative, *Mahzor for Rosh Hashanah and Yom Kippur* (1978); and Orthodox, *The Complete*

ArtScroll Machzor (1990). In *Justice and Mercy: Commentary on the Liturgy of the New Year and the Day of Atonement* (1963), Max Arzt adds valuable background. The Nobel Prize–winning Israeli author, S. Y. Agnon, produced a now-classic treasury of traditions, legends, and commentaries on Rosh Hashanah and Yom Kippur, translated into English as *Days of Awe* (1965). On the question of why good people suffer, the place to start is Rabbi Harold Kushner's classic on that subject: *When Bad Things Happen to Good People* (1981).

Many of the books for Rosh Hashanah also cover the themes of Yom Kippur. For the special liturgy that describes the Yom Kippur service in the Ancient Temple, see Michael D. Swartz and Joseph Yahalom, eds., *Avodah: An Anthology of Ancient Poetry for Yom Kippur* (2005). The classic book on Jewish community is Salo Baron, *The Jewish Community: Its History and Structure to the American Revolution* (3 vols., 1945). Daniel Elazar, in *Community and Polity: The Organizational Dynamics of American Jewry* (1976, 1995), analyzes the Jewish community of the United States. His *People and Polity: Organizational Dynamics of World Jewry* (1979) covers the rest of the world. For key concepts that underlie the Jewish view of community, see Sol Roth, *The Jewish Idea of Community* (1977).

There are lots of illustrations of award-winning sukkot on the Internet; for a volume of photographs based on a museum exhibit, see *A Moveable Feast: Sukkahs from Around the World* (2003). The idea of *ḥesed* is discussed in Warren Zev Levy, "Grace or Loving-kindness," in Arthur A. Cohen and Paul Mendes Flohr, *Contemporary Jewish Religious Thought* (1987). For the idea of *tikkun olam*, see Emil Fackenheim, *To Mend the World: Foundations of Future Jewish Thought* (1982); Elliot Dorff, *The Way into Tikkun Olam* (2005); and David Shatz, Chaim I. Waxman, and Nathan J. Diament, eds., *Tikkun Olam: Social Responsibility in Jewish Thought and Law* (1997).

The Book of Maccabees, found in the Apocrypha (so-called hidden books that were not included in the Bible), sets forth the basic story of Ḥanukkah. *The Apocrypha of the Old Testament: Revised Standard Version*, edited by Bruce Metzger (1977), contains all four books of the Maccabees. *I Maccabees* (1976) and *II Maccabees* (1983) by Jonathan Goldstein are unsurpassed. For the entire period, see W. D. Davies and Louis Finkelstein, eds., *The Cambridge History of Judaism: The Hellenistic Age* (1989). On the holiday in America and its relationship to Christmas, see Jenna W. Joselit, "Merry Chanukah: The Changing Holiday Practices of American Jews, 1880–1950," in Jack Wertheimer, ed., *The Uses of Tradition* (1993); and Jonathan D. Sarna, "Is Judaism Compatible with American Civil Religion? The Problem of Christmas and the 'National Faith'"; in Rowland A. Sherrill, ed., *Religion and the Life of the Nation* (1990). There are reams of popular articles on all aspects of

Jewish-Christian intermarriage. For book-length studies, see Egon Mayer, *Love and Tradition: Marriage Between Jews and Christians* (1985); Sylvia Barack Fishman, *Double or Nothing: Jewish Families and Mixed Marriage* (2004); and Keren McGinity, *Still Jewish: A History of Women and Intermarriage in America* (2008).

The literature on Judaism and the environment is relatively new and therefore particularly worth pondering on Tu bi-Shevat (and today!). *Trees, Earth and Torah: A Tu B'Shvat Anthology*, edited by Ari Elon, Naomi Mara Hyman, and Arthur Waskow (2000), displays the new environmental focus of the holiday along with other Tu bi-Shevat traditions. Havah Tirosh-Samuelson, in *Judaism and Ecology: Created World and Revealed Word* (2003); Martin Yaffe, in *Judaism and Environmental Ethics: A Reader* (2001); and Manfred Gerstenfeld, in *Judaism, Environmentalism and the Environment: Mapping and Analysis* (1998), present scholarly materials concerning Jewish attitudes toward environmental issues. For more popular approaches, see Ellen Bernstein, *Ecology and the Jewish Spirit: Where Nature and the Sacred Meet* (2000); and Jeremy Benstein, *The Way into Judaism and the Environment* (2006).

The highly readable biblical book of Esther tells the basic story of Purim. For modern commentaries and studies, see Adele Berlin, *Esther: The JPS Bible Commentary* (2001); Jon Levenson, *Esther: A Commentary* (1997); and Michael V. Fox, *Character and Ideology in the Book of*

Esther (2001). For a traditional commentary based on rabbinic sources, see Meir Zlotowitz, *Esther: The Megillah* (1976). In *Every Person's Guide to Purim* (2000), Ronald H. Isaacs offers a fine selection of customs and traditions. For a description of one Hasidic Purim play, see Shifra Epstein, "Drama on a Table: The Bobover Hasidim Piremshpiyl," in Harvey Goldberg, ed., *Judaism Viewed from Within and from Without* (1987). On the broader question—how to survive as a Jew—thousands of different books provide hundreds of different answers. A readable book with a wonderful title is Ronald A. Brauner, *Being Jewish in a Gentile World: A Survival Guide* (2000).

NOTES

CHAPTER 1

3   **Besides, they ask:** Adele Berlin and Marc Zvi Brettler, eds., *The Jewish Study Bible* (New York: Oxford University Press, 2004), p. 104.

5   **"Where do we find":** J. Leonard Levy, *Haggadah or Home Service for the Festival of Passover*, 7th ed. (Pittsburgh: Rodef Shalom Congregation, 1922; original ed., 1903), pp. 25–27.

7   **Some fifty million copies:** Carole B. Balin, "'Good to the Last Drop': The Proliferation of the Maxwell House Haggadah," *My People's Passover Haggadah*, edited by Lawrence A. Hoffman and David Arnow (Woodstock, VT: Jewish Lights Publishing, 2008), p. 85.

14   **"We've made another Seder":** This translation of the Hebrew song "Ḥasal Sidur Pesaḥ" is modified from two texts: David Geffen, ed., *American Heritage Haggadah* (Jerusalem: Geffen, 1992), 81; and Jonathan Saks, *Rabbi Jonathan Sacks's Haggadah* (New York: Continuum, 2006), p. 99.

CHAPTER 2

19   **The festival, back then:** See Harvey E. Goldberg, "The Mimuna and the Minority Status of Moroccan Jews," *Ethnology* 17, no. 1. (January 1978), pp. 75–87.

23   **"You are a people consecrated to the Lord your God":** Deuteronomy 7: 6–8. Unless otherwise stated, all biblical translations are based on the Jewish Publication Society translation, *Tanakh* (Philadelphia: Jewish Publication Society, 1985, 1999).

24   **The Jewish philosopher Martin Buber:** *A Land of Two Peoples: Buber on Jews and Arabs*, edited by Paul Mendes-Flohr (New York: Oxford University Press, 1983), p. 56.

CHAPTER 3

32   **"For the first time":** Abba Kovner, *Scrolls of Testimony*, translated by Eddie Levenston (Philadelphia: Jewish Publication Society, 2001), p. 6.

35   **"There were 30,000 of us":** *We Are Children Just the Same: "Vedem": The Secret Magazine by the Boys of Terezín.* Prepared and selected from the magazine *In the Lead* (Vedem) by Marie Ruth Křížková, Kurt Jiří Koutouč, and Zdeněk Ornest; translated from the Czech by R. Elizabeth Novak ; edited by Paul R. Wilson; with a foreword by Václav Havel (Philadelphia: Jewish Publication Society, 1995), p. 88.

37   **"I believe in the sun":** Quoted in Marcia Sachs Littell, ed., *Liturgies on the Holocaust: An Interfaith Anthology* (Philadelphia: Anne Frank Institute, 1986), p. 122.

39   **"Do not mourn too much":** *Megilat ha-Sho'ah—The Shoah Scroll: A Holocaust Liturgy*, translated by Jules Har-

low (Jerusalem: Rabbinical Assembly/Schechter Institute for Jewish Studies, 2004), p. 57.

CHAPTER 4

46   **"His Majesty's Government":** Balfour Declaration, November 2, 1917, reprinted in Itamar Rabinovich and Jehuda Reinharz, eds., *Israel in the Middle East*, 2nd ed. (Waltham: Brandeis University Press, 2008), p. 29.

47   **"We, the members of the National Council":** Israel's Declaration of Independence, in ibid., pp. 72–74.

48   **Even after "being forcibly exiled":** Ibid, p. 72.

48   **"THE STATE OF ISRAEL will be open":** Ibid., p. 73.

49   **"This will be a war of extermination":** Azzam Pasha, as quoted in Howard M. Sachar, *A History of Israel from the Rise of Zionism to Our Time* (New York: Knopf, 1976), p. 333.

51   **"Well, the neighborhood bully":** Bob Dylan, *Infidels*, copyright © 1983 Special Rider Music. Reprinted by permission.

53   **The fact that this might lead:** Alvin Rosenfeld, *"Progressive" Jewish Thought and the New Anti-Semitism* (New York: American Jewish Committee, 2006).

54   **"Criticizing Israel":** Thomas L. Friedman, "Campus Hypocrisy," *New York Times*, October 16, 2002, p. 27.

54   **"He who reproves his neighbor":** Babylonian Talmud, Tractate Tamid, p. 28a.

56   **"Cause Your spirit's influence":** *Kol Haneshamah Shabbat VeHagim* (Wyncote, PA: Reconstructionist Press, 1994), pp. 420–421.

CHAPTER 5

59   **"On Friday, the sixth day":** Cecil Roth, "The Torah's Marriage in Gibraltar," in Philip Goodman, ed., *The Shavuot Anthology* (Philadelphia: Jewish Publication Society, 1974), pp. 156–157; cf. 99–101.

62   **"Just as a hammer":** Babylonian Talmud, Tractate Sanhedrin, p. 34a.

63   **A devoted student:** Nahum M. Sarna, *The JPS Torah Commentary: Genesis* (Philadelphia: Jewish Publication Society, 1989), p. xv.

63   **"Desert me for one day":** Jerusalem Talmud, Tractate Berahot, p. 94b (Vilna ed., p. 68a).

64   **"I acknowledge this day":** Deuteronomy 26:3, 5–10.

65   **In the play:** Midrash Exodus Rabbah 27:9, as reprinted in Philip Goodman, ed., *The Shavuot Anthology* (Philadelphia: Jewish Publication Society, 1974), p. 38.

66   **No people has a monopoly:** Mekhilta de-Rabbi Ishmael on Exodus 20:2 in ibid., p. 39.

67   **"Gather the people":** Deuteronomy 31:12.

68   **Even a brief period:** Isaac ben Eliakim of Posen, *Lev Tov* (1620), as excerpted in Simcha Assaf, *Mekorot le-toldhot ha-Hinukh be-Yisrael*, ed. Shmuel Glick (New York: Jewish Theological Seminary, 2002), vol. 1, pp. 556–559.

68   **"He who teaches his daughter Torah":** Mishnah Sotah, 3:4.

68   **"Most women's minds":** Moses Maimonides, *Laws of Torah Study*, 1:1, 1:13.

68   **"Not only is it *permitted*":** Rabbi Zalman Sorotzkin, *Moznayim la-Mishpat*, 1955, sec. 42, as quoted in *Encyclopaedia Judaica*, 2nd ed. (Jerusalem: Keter Publishing

House, 2007), vol. 21, p. 200. All subsequent references to this encyclopedia refer to the second edition.

70 **"By denying yourself sleep":** Louis Jacobs, *Jewish Mystical Testimonies* (New York: Schocken Books, 1976), p. 100.

72 **Some wanted that monument removed:** *Van Orden v. Perry* 125 S.Ct. 2722 (2005).

75 **"Study is greater":** Babylonian Talmud, Tractate Kiddushin, p. 40b.

CHAPTER 6

77 **"Alas," the book declares:** Lamentations 1:1–2.

79 **That is the clear message:** Lamentations 1:8.

79 **"Sometimes," as the Bible acknowledges:** Ecclesiastes 7:15.

80 **A strong, vibrant Judaism:** See Dennis Prager and Joseph Telushkin, *Why the Jews: The Reason for Antisemitism* (New York: Simon and Schuster, 1983).

80 **As far back as the Bible:** Numbers 23:9, Esther 3:8.

81 **"Oh: that I might weep continuously":** Abraham Rosenfeld, *The Authorised Kinot for the Ninth of Av* (New York: Judaica Press, 1979), p. 132; I have modified the translation.

83 **The destruction of Jerusalem:** *Encyclopaedia Judaica*, vol. 2, p. 716; see David Einhorn, *Olat Tamid: Book of Prayers for Israelitish Congregations* (New York: E. Thalmessinger, 1872), pp. 330–333.

84 **"May all who mourn Jerusalem":** This new version of the classic prayer, *Nahem*, was composed by Professor Ephraim E. Urbach after the Six-Day War; a copy is in

the author's possession and the translation from Hebrew is mine.

CHAPTER 7

90 **As part of the day's festivities:** Babylonian Talmud, Tractate Taanit, pp. 26b, 30b–31a.

90 **Jewish tradition:** Midrash Genesis Rabbah, Bereshit, pp. xvii, 2; for this and similar quotations in English, see C. G. Montefiore and H. Loewe, *A Rabbinic Anthology* (New York: Schocken, 1974), pp. 507–508.

91 **Real happiness:** Ethics of the Fathers 5:21.

92 **The rate of success:** Babylonian Talmud, Tractate Sotah, p. 2a.

92 **And even then:** *New York Times*, July 1, 2007, Styles Section; Egon Mayer, *American Jewish Identity Survey* (New York: 2001), 26; for the Boston Jewish community study, see http://www.cjp.org/local_includes/downloads/16072 .pdf, p. 11.

93 **The conclusion of the study:** *The National Jewish Population Survey 2000–2001* (New York: United Jewish Communities, 2003), pp. 3–4.

CHAPTER 8

98 **The book of Numbers:** Numbers 29:1.

99 **By their calculation:** *Encyclopaedia Judaica*, vol. 4, p. 796.

100 **Ten days later:** This brief selection from the traditional high holiday hymn, "U-Netanneh Tokef," is from the translation of Reuven Hammer, *Entering the High Holy Days* (Philadelphia: Jewish Publication Society, 1998), p. 87.

102 **However much God may foresee:** Ethics of the Fathers 3:15.

102 **He recalled the story:** Babylonian Talmud, Tractate Rosh Hashanah, p. 16b.

105 **"The ethical component of Rosh Hashanah":** http://www.csjo.org/pages/holidays/roshhashanah.htm.

105 **Like Abraham in the Bible:** Genesis 18:25.

105 **Once, New Year's Day had dominated my life:** Elie Wiesel, *Night*, translated by Stella Rodway (New York: Hill and Wang, 1960), pp. 72–74.

107 **God alone knows:** This translation is from Ben Zion Bokser, *The High Holiday Prayer Book* (New York: Hebrew Publishing Company, 1959), p. 271.

CHAPTER 9

111 **"On this day shall atonement":** Leviticus 16:30.

112 **"We abuse, we betray, we are cruel":** Translation of Ashamnu, by Rabbi Jules Harlow, reprinted from the *Mahzor for Rosh Hashanah and Yom Kippur*, edited by Rabbi Jules Harlow, copyright © 1972 by the Rabbinical Assembly, p. 403.

112 **For all of these:** Ben Zion Bokser, *The High Holiday Prayer Book* (New York: Hebrew Publishing Company, 1959), p. 293.

113 **"I don't regard the Jewish people":** Joey Kurtzman, "The Coming Jewish Schism," www.jewcy.com/node/6809/print.

113 **"I have a special responsibility":** Jonathan D. Sarna, *American Judaism: A History* (New Haven: Yale University Press, 2004), pp. 363–364.

115 **That is what Jews pray for:** Joseph H. Hertz, *The Authorized Daily Prayer Book* (New York: Bloch Publishing, 1948), p. 211.

116 **Wasn't I the person:** Samuel G. Freedman, *Jew vs. Jew: The Struggle for the Soul of American Jewry* (New York: Simon & Schuster, 2000).

118 **"The communal atonement":** Arnold Lustiger, ed., *Yom Kippur Machzor, with Commentary from the Teachings of Rabbi Joseph Soloveitchik* (New York: K'hal Publishing, 2006), p. 66, italics added.

119 **The day is described:** Lamentations Rabbah 33, in Philip Goodman, *The Yom Kippur Anthology* (Philadelphia: Jewish Publication Society, 1971), p. 23.

119 **We may enter the day feeling guilty:** Pesikta Rabbati 40:5 in ibid, p. 25.

119 **"For transgressions":** Mishnah Yoma 8:9.

120 **"Truth," the president of Harvard University recently observed:** http://www.president.harvard.edu/speeches/faust/071012_installation.html.

121 **An ancient rabbinic homily:** William G. Braude and Israel J. Kapstein, *Tanna Děbē Eliyyahu: The Lore of the School of Elijah* (Philadelphia: Jewish Publication Society, 1981), p. 516.

121 **God forgives "iniquity, transgression, and sin":** Exodus 34:7.

CHAPTER 10

123 **"You shall live in Sukkot":** Leviticus 23:42.

124 **God personally set forth:** Ibid., 23:43.

126 **It is well in wealth:** Philo, *Special Laws* 2.204, in Philip Goodman, *The Sukkot/Simḥat Torah Anthology* (Philadelphia: Jewish Publication Society, 1988), p. 15.

126 **In addition, Philo gleans:** Ibid., p. 14.

127 **According to one of the medieval Jewish Bible commentators:** Rashbam commentary on Leviticus 23:43, as translated in ibid., p. 54.

128 **It privileges needs, not rights:** Ibid., p. 302.

129 **It demanded prayer:** Lawrence Fine, "Tikkun: A Lurianic Motif in Contemporary Jewish Thought," in Jacob Neusner et al., *From Ancient Israel to Modern Judaism: Essays in Honor of Marvin Fox* (Atlanta: Scholars Press, 1989), pp. 35–53.

129 **God's world:** Leonard Fein, *Where Are We: The Inner Life of America's Jews* (New York: Harper & Row, 1988), p. 198.

131 **For a blessing and not for a curse:** Hermann Naphtali Adler, *Service of the Synagogue: Tabernacles* (New York: Hebrew Publishing, n.d.), p. 139.

132 **Nor do most:** Goodman, *Sukkot/Simḥat Torah Anthology*, p. 42.

132 **"The other righteous men and women":** Adler, *Service of the Synagogue*, p. 127a (translation mine).

134 **"A time to every purpose":** Ecclesiastes 3:1.

CHAPTER 11

136 **"All should be one people":** 1 Maccabees 1:41–42.

137 **"Even if all the nations":** I Maccabees 2: 19–22, 27.

137 **More broadly, it kept:** *Encyclopaedia Judaica*, vol. 8, p. 446.

140 **Rather than choosing:** http://www.chrismukkah.com/content/merry_mazel_tov/ghosts_of_chrismukkah_past/about.html.

142 **Some twenty-five hundred years ago:** Nehemiah 10:31.

142 **As a result, the taboo:** Jonathan D. Sarna, "Intermarriage in America: The Jewish Experience in Historical Context," in Stuart Cohen and Bernard Susser, eds., *Ambivalent Jew: Charles Liebman in Memoriam* (New York: Jewish Theological Seminary, 2007), pp. 125–133.

143 **As a group, they assimilated:** *Encyclopaedia Judaica*, vol. 6, p. 608.

143 **Today, Jamaica boasts:** Carol Holzberg, *Minorities and Power in a Black Society: The Jewish Community of Jamaica* (Lanham, MD: University Press of America, 1987), p. 20; Mordecai Arbell, *The Jewish Nation of the Caribbean* (Jerusalem: Geffen, 2002), pp. 225–260.

144 **Given the estimate of 5.3 million Jews currently in the United States:** *American Jewish Year Book* 107 (2007), p. 507.

CHAPTER 12

148 **"On the fifteenth of Shevat":** http://www.akhlah.com/holidays/tubshvat/seder/hagaddah.php.

149 **If one walnut is removed:** Midrash Shir HaShirim Rabah 6:11.

150 **One of my students:** Genesis 1:28.

151 **"The Holy Blessed One":** Midrash Ecclesiastes Rabbah 7:13, as cited and translated in *Encyclopaedia Judaica*, vol. 6, p. 449.

151 **The book of Deuteronomy:** Deuteronomy 20:19.

151 **"Whoever breaks vessels":** Maimonides, Laws of Kings 6:10.

151 **Another rabbi insisted:** Sefer Ha-Ḥinnukh (Jerusalem: Mossad HaRav Kook, 1954), p. 647, commandment 530.

151 **Rabbi Joseph:** Ethics of the Fathers 3:9.

152 **"It is not the expression":** Nosson Scherman et al., eds., *The Complete ArtScroll Siddur* (New York: ArtScroll, 1987), p. 560.

152 **"These are essential":** Abraham Maimonides, as quoted at http://www.coejl.org/jewviro.php.

152 **Laws passed to protect:** See the ruling of Rabbi Solomon b. Adret, as cited in *Encyclopedia Judaica*, vol. 6, p. 95.

153 **"For Jews, the environmental crisis":** http://www.coejl .org/~coejlor/about/founding.php.

CHAPTER 13

155 **Casting lots:** Esther 3:13.

156 **The result is the very first:** Esther 9:23.

158 **"I will utterly blot out":** Exodus 17: 14–16; Deuteronomy 25: 17–19.

INDEX